LIVING *the* MIRACLE

HOW I LEARNED *to* SEE THE MIRACLES *along* MY JOURNEY *through* CANCER

DURELL TUBERVILLE

HIGH BRIDGE BOOKS
HOUSTON

Living the Miracle
by Durell Tuberville

Copyright © 2015 by Durell Tuberville
All rights reserved.

Printed in the United States of America
ISBN (Paperback): 978-1-940024-59-2
ISBN (eBook): 978-1-940024-58-5

High Bridge Books titles may be purchased in bulk for educational, business, fundraising, or sales promotional use. For information please contact High Bridge Books via www.HighBridgeBooks.com/contact.

Published in Houston, Texas by High Bridge Books

CONTENTS

SPECIAL THANKS

I owe a great deal of gratitude to my wife Susan who has walked this journey with me. She has been my greatest support and confidant. Definitely the journey would have been more difficult if I had to navigate it by myself. She assisted not only with the writing and original draft, but in the living of the miracles that are the subjects of this book. Thank you, Susan.

Secondly, a special thank you to Patti Bornaman. It was Patti who heard the leading of God's Spirit to encourage me to begin this project. Patti also volunteered to conduct the initial interviews and transcribe those interviews into the first draft. She labored many hours organizing chapters, interviewing me, and transcribing the interviews. This would not have happened without Patti. Thank you, Patti.

—Durell

AN OPENING WORD

from Craig Kennedy

I have known Durell since about 2004. Around that time, the Lord was calling me into the chaplaincy, but I had a hard time realizing it. One night at a Gideon's dinner, when I heard that they gave Bibles to Emergency Responders, my heart went out to a friend of mine who is an emergency responder. God spoke to my heart right then and there, "I want you to be a Chaplain," but for a while I fought the thought. Finally, I wound up having a couple conversations with people about my experience, and one of them, Paul Navarre, told me he had just recently had a conversation with Durell Tuberville, the Shreveport Fire Department Chaplain, who happened to be looking for someone to mentor in the field of chaplaincy.

Within two weeks, I met Durell, received a Fire Department identification badge, and started learning to become an emergency service chaplain. I have worked with Durell ever since. We worked off and on together for about four years, and then in 2008, he offered me the opportunity to come on board with Personal Solutions, Inc. At the time this writing, I have worked full time with him for a little over six years. I would never be able to share all that Durell has taught me over these years. As anyone who knows him knows, there is no one like Durell, a one of a kind individual.

The first time I made a fire scene with him, I scratched my head as I watched him interact with the firemen, who were soaking wet and covered in smut and ash. None of it fazed Durell. One particular fireman walked up to give him a dirty, wet, smut-black hug; then Durell turned around and gave him a kiss! I wondered, "What have I got myself into?" I don't do *that*! But Durell does! He *can*!

Durell has also shown me how to look beyond what a person says on the surface to what they are really saying in their heart. I think we, as human beings, look at each other on the surface and talk to each other on the surface so much that the surface is all we can focus on. Durell, on the other hand, has the amazing gift to see what is being said behind the words. He loves people enough to listen to what they are really saying.

I have met very few people who have the faith and interaction with God that Durell has. A personal example of this occurred during a family crisis of my own. When I received the call to work in chaplaincy, I left my full-time job at the plant (and this was before I came to work with Durell full-time), but my wife still worked. One day, I got a call from my wife saying that she had lost her job! As I was heading out to go to her, my phone rang. It was Durell. Now, if you have ever met Durell, you know he is all about the relationship. How are you? How is your spouse? How are your kids? How are your parents? The introduction to a conversation with Durell is about five minutes long because he wants to make sure everybody in your world is ok. But on this day as soon as I answered the phone, Durell said to me, "What just happened?" as if he knew something was wrong. When I told him, he said he had been awakened by the Spirit early that morning and began to pray for Melissa and me because he knew something was about to happen. At that very moment, he had stepped out in between meetings, and God told him to call me right then! Whatever had happened, he needed to talk to me.

Durell has that ability to listen and hear God with no fear of acting upon what he thinks God is telling him. I knew he was special before, but on that day, I began to see just how special and just how deep his faith runs.

Durell also has the ability to call to mind and speak the Word of God so vividly for every new situation he faces. On a moment's notice, he can recall a Scripture for anything you are going through. I admire this so much.

Durell has always been positive. He *is* human: he gets frustrated at times, angry at times, but rarely have I heard him say anything negative about anyone because his outlook is always so positive. With people or with situations, he always sees where the good can come out of it. I heard a pastor say one time, that as Christians, we should not say we "failed," but rather we should say we have "fallen." I believe Durell sees situations just like that. He looks at every situation and says, "I can do something different next time." If he makes a mistake, he does not count himself out. He just figures it did not work out right then. That is how he views his life, that is how he views his business, and that is how he views the people he comes in contact with.

When he told me he had been diagnosed with cancer, it was a shock! I guess the best way to describe it was surreal. I did not know how to respond. I didn't know what to do. All of us here at the office felt he had done so much for us that now it was our time to take care of him, to make sure everything that he had put into this business—and our lives—did not go under just because he was suddenly sick. So it didn't. It did tighten our focus a bit, but we tightened our belts and began to live the miracle with him.

As his cancer journey began, Durell's thoughts seemed to be, "I am going to stay as normal as possible." He planned to keep doing all the things he had done on a daily basis before the diagnosis. We just knew that was what he would try to do, but it proved not to be possible. That presented a learning curve for him and us. I think the treatments took more of a toll on him than he would allow himself to express. He never said that, but you could tell. There were times early on when we had to make him go home because he was still trying to do too much. We would cancel appointments but tell him he just did not have any; that way he could go home early. He never refused our efforts, but it is equally true that he never initiated cancelling appointments himself. He just would not bring himself to do that, so cancellations were something we had to help him do.

I know he is a crisis and trauma specialist and trainer, but it was through his own crisis that he taught us the most. One of the most powerful comparisons I can think of after watching Durell go through this painful time is in the movie, *Passion of the Christ*. One of the most telling scenes of that movie is when Christ is tied to a post face down, beaten and whipped with the forty lashes. As it was portrayed in the movie, all Christ did between beatings was stand back up. He did not say anything. He didn't moan; he didn't groan; he didn't whine. He simply stood up. The tormentors didn't quite know what to do. So they beat him again. I saw this kind of response in Durell during his battle with cancer. He certainly did not like cancer, but you never heard him say anything about it. If you did hear him get a little riled, it would be more about the situational challenges than the cancer itself. For instance, when he could not ride his motorcycle anymore, he would say, "Cancer sucks!" But that was because he couldn't ride his motorcycle. He was not bemoaning the fact that he had cancer. He was simply frustrated because he couldn't go ride his motorcycle. I saw that was to be the way he would embrace his cancer.

Durell once made a statement I will always hold close. Just the two of us were in the office one day when he looked at me with eyes a little moist and said, "How blessed am I that God chose me to have cancer so that I can go through this, and someone can hear about the love of Christ through my journey?" Durell is probably the only person I have heard of in this type of situation to say how blessed he is! That was his mindset throughout the entire journey. He considered himself blessed because he felt his story could be used to reach other people.

It was amazing to see through this journey how many people Durell has influenced. Everywhere I go throughout our community, people would ask, "How is Durell doing?" It was kind of funny in a way because when you ask about someone who has Stage Four cancer, you usually ask with a gloomy look on your face, with compassionate doom in your voice, so it became somewhat fun to answer them, "Man, he is great! He hasn't lost any hair. He has even gained weight!" All the usual reports did not apply to Durell. People would look at me bewildered and amazed. When Durell would show up at an event, people would say after he had left the scene, "Oh, he looks so good." He did look good. Other than during the months with the episodes of C-diff, he did not look sick at all.

Durell taught through example how we should face trials and challenges in our own lives. Our response to challenges should not be "Woe is me," but rather, "How blessed am I that I can go through this and it can touch someone for Christ?" Durell taught us that. He has definitely caused me to expand the territories of my thinking and the comfort zones of my world. I hope when you read Living the Miracle, you will meet the same Durell we all know and love. And I hope this book helps you the way knowing Durell has helped me.

INTRODUCTION

I was raised in Keithville, Louisiana and graduated high school here in Caddo Parish. Growing up I always thought I would follow in my father's footsteps and become a general contractor specializing in residential construction.

However, after marrying the girl of my dreams, I was face to face with the fact that I did not know how to be a very good husband. Working and providing was easy. It was relationship that I struggled with. Later I found out that most all my friends were not good at it either.

Susan, my wife, told me I needed to determine if I wanted to be single, running the woods, fishing, and hanging out with the guys or if I wanted to be married. I wanted to be married but did not really know how to do that very well.

Soon after that conversation, Susan came home with the news that she was pregnant. Wow, how that hit me square in the face because I began to evaluate the characteristics and values I wanted my son to have. I could not come up with many. The only thing I could think to do was to go to the God my mom and wife had been praying for me to approach.

So, in August of 1979 sitting on the front porch of 2622 Lakehurst Street in Shreveport, Louisiana, looking into the vast night sky full of brilliant stars, I ask God to forgive me of my sins and pledged to live for Him the rest of my life. He did and I am.

The following November 06, our oldest son Josh was born and more than anything, I wanted him to have a good father. So I began to seek God through our church, and the Bible to gain the knowledge to become a God man.

Susan and I moved from Shreveport in 1980 to attend Bible College and the ministry of Jesus Christ began in our lives and remains to this day. It was here that our second son was born, Dustin. Living for God became my passion even more now that two sons were depending on me to show them how to live as a God man.

We have served as dorm directors at college, youth pastors in two cities, senior pastor for ten years, associate pastor and counselor at our church, and emergency service fire and police chaplain for twenty seven years. Our lives became living servants for the cause of the gospel of Jesus Christ.

I completed my education with a bachelor's degree in Pastoral Ministry, a master's degree in counseling and a PhD in Human Services to better minister to those emergency responders God placed me with. I started my counseling practice in 1993 and it remains to this day. Susan and I have a mediation business that does domestic and civil mediation as a business to give to God's work. We have a property management business for our retirement and work with a variety of community agencies as a volunteer and supporter.

I specialize in trauma counseling and have served as the coordinator for critical incident stress following the Murrah building bombing in Oklahoma City in 1995. Our CISM team went there at the request of our Fire Chief Bo Roberts and served eleven days coordinating teams from all over the country and handing it off to OKC Fire Department on the eighth day following the bombing.

I also coordinated the Crisis Intervention program for the Louisiana Department of Health and Hospitial's Bureau of Emergency Medical Service for six weeks immediately following Hurricanes Katrina and Rita. So, as you can see, I am an adrenaline junkie.

Susan and I are complete opposites that bring perfect balance to our relationship and have since we were twelve years old. Yes that's right we started "going steady" when we were twelve and have been together for the past 44 years, married 38 of those years. She is the balance I need every day of my life and God has used her as my care provider during my struggle with cancer.

September 28, 2012, the doctor called my office to inform me of the outcome of a series of MRI's and CT scans. I had a rectal mass, a rectal tumor, determined to be rectal adenocarcinoma. At that very moment, life began to change. There was no way of knowing all that I was about to face, or what to do about it.

This particular point in time brought me to the question I never thought I would have to answer, "How am I going to live through cancer? What am I going to do with a diagnosis like this?" The only way I could see living through something this big was to visualize the end result exactly how I would want it to be, then—to live that vision. Seeing myself as healed was the only way I could be successful.

I quickly chose to view this diagnosis the way I view riding a motorcycle. When I get into a really tight corner, the only way I can negotiate that corner with any success is to look for the thrill of victory, to look at where I am headed, instead of looking at the present position I am in. To stare directly into the corner would bring about disaster, but to look around the corner as far as I can see and to push myself to that point always gets me through.

In order for me not to 'crash and burn' with this devastating diagnosis, I had to begin to look forward. As I peered beyond the corner and into my future, I asked myself a simple question, "What's my mantra going to be? What can I say to myself over and over again to get through this trial?" Only one answer rang back to my heart, and it rang so true that I knew it would last— "I am going to LIVE a MIRACLE. I am going to be the one who allows God to do His thing in my life. My part is simply to go on being me."

That evening at home as I was making my commitment to God—"I am going to continue to live for You, God"—I asked the question, "Why not me?" Not the question, "Why do I have cancer?" or "How could this happen to me?" but rather, "How am I going to live through this process; how am I going to LIVE?" I decided then and there, not one day would pass that I don't call upon God to do the healing. I would not let one day go by without declaring the glory of God. I would never close another letter, or any correspondence, without a mantra that gives glory to God. I would continue to focus on what God can do, not on my circumstances. I would, indeed, see the smooth road on the other end of the tight curve and make plans to get there.

So, while I was at home standing on my front porch, I said, "I am going to live the miracle!"

That same night, I called my pastor, Denny Duron, to tell him I had been diagnosed with rectal adenocarcinoma. He asked, "What do you want to do? What can I help you do?" I said, "Help me live the miracle. I am going to Live the Miracle." And from that day on, I decided I am Living the Miracle. Every day, I am living the miracle. That statement has become my mantra.

Now, anyone who knows me has heard the phrase "Living the Miracle." It is the focus that's gotten me through the curve. It has become my refrain in this cancer-fighting endeavor. Every day of my life, I tell somebody, or a group of people, that I am Living the Miracle.

Every day since that diagnosis, many times a day, I remind myself that I am living the miracle for God. Every chance I have, I remind others, too. I even stop several times a day to remind God that I am living this miracle for His glory, for Him.

One hundred years from now, nobody is going to remember Durell Tuberville, but what they might remember is the story of the guy who 'Lived the Miracle,' proclaiming God's goodness throughout dire circumstances. This story is how he lived the miracle called life. This is how that guy stayed positive. This is how he stayed the course.

Does Durell Tuberville keep a 'bucket list' (to borrow a term coined by a popular movie)? Yes, there are plenty of things I want to do. However, the things I hope to "do" are not the sum of who

I am. Who I am is a man from God desiring to be the best I can be, to do my best to overlook my many past failures and live the rest of my life, regardless of how many days that may be, solely focusing on being the best I can be for the glory of God.

I am Living the Miracle. That's how I came by the title of this book. Living the Miracle is not for me but rather for God. Living the Miracle through cancer to enable others to be encouraged and motivated to live the miracle, too, that is my goal. That is what keeps me going.

It is my hope that as you read Living the Miracle, you will be blessed and inspired to recognize the Miracles of God all around you and continue to live your Miracle as well.

Living the Miracle,
J. Durell Tuberville

CHAPTER 1

THE MIRACLE OF THE DIAGNOSIS

I had a colonoscopy in April of 2012. It was the first colonoscopy I had ever had. I was fifty-four years old at the time.

Every Thursday morning for many years running, I have met with a group of old friends. We have book studies and talk about (or laugh about) things that affect us as old men. We also discuss how to deal with these issues, employing God's principles as best as we can. This group is sort of an accountability group, and it was two of these dear friends who had encouraged me (or goaded me) to have this colonoscopy.

Through much trepidation, I finally agreed to schedule it because I knew I had internal hemorrhoid problems. I cannot tell you why this particular procedure created such anxiety for me except that I was completely ignorant of how a colonoscopy works. I find most men are that way. We create false fear out of thin air and avoid examinations to our own peril. When I finally learned about the procedure and focused on reality, I overcame the fear and set the appointment.

My doctor did not report any abnormalities or unusual polyps at that time, only that there were three hemorrhoids, a fact I had already expected to hear. After these results, I went on with life as normal, understanding that simple banding procedures would soon be necessary to correct the hemorrhoid problem. These procedures were scheduled separately for each necessary banding—May, June, and July of 2012. I would definitely call the first two banding procedures uncomfortable, but the third one registered as VERY painful. I told the doctor at the time of the procedure about the increase in pain when he banded the third hemorrhoid as compared to the other two. It was painful enough for me to break out in a sweat and groan. The doctor explained that the hemorrhoid was large and the band was low but the pain should dissipate in a few hours, if not sooner. He was right. In a few hours, it went through its due process and worked out fine.

A few weeks later, however, another issue surfaced. I was having some stream problems, so I set an appointment to see my urologist. We already knew about and had been dealing with a benign enlarged prostate, but my urologist concluded this stream issue called for an up-to-date digital exam. It was this doctor and his digits that saved the day by recognizing the tumor in my colon. When he began the exam, it was unexpectedly painful! When I told him so, he said "No, it is uncomfortable, but not painful." I argued with him saying, "No, it hurts!" Then he asked, "On the pain scale of 1 to 10, where is it?" "Well, about a 5," I rated it. A five was more than I had anticipated this examination to cause and far more than he said it should. Of course, he concurred that my prostate was indeed enlarged, but his next words led to a much more painful discovery: "That [enlarged prostate] is not my main concern." As he began to extract his finger, he came to the tumor area which up until this moment, I didn't know existed. "*This* is my concern," he said as he pressed on the tumor.

Pain shot to about an 8, as I broke into a sweat, buckling at the knees! If I hadn't had something to hold on to, surely I would have gone to the floor. "That really hurt?" the doctor asked. I exclaimed, "Yes, sir, it really did!"

That was on a Friday. My urologist immediately telephoned my G.I. doctor and requested a lower sigmoid colonoscopy. The following Monday we had the procedure done.

On Wednesday, September 28, 2012, the G.I. doctor called me and confirmed I definitely had rectal cancer. He told me I needed to find a rectal surgeon, and upon my request, recommended a great doctor from our area, whom I immediately called to make an appointment.

In the meantime, I contacted an oncologist whom I have known for years, a fine man with a stellar reputation. Since I am a trauma therapist, Dr. Bob (as he is affectionately known and will be referred to from here on in my story) had previously referred oncology patients to me, patients who were dealing with grief or end of life issues. He and his wife Lisa have been treating oncology patients for many years and I was fortunate to be able to work alongside of them. Because of these connections, I already had a great working relationship with him and his staff, so when I asked him if he could treat my type of cancer, I was very glad to hear, "Yes." Then, I asked if he would be my medical oncologist, to which he added, "Absolutely!"

With all of this underway, Susan and I went to see the colorectal surgeon. His exam and review of the CT scan concurred with the cancer diagnosis, so we immediately began to discuss our medical options and strategies. Surgery would be a necessity and the first move toward ridding my body of this tumor. Surgery, however, meant I would be left with a permanent colostomy. The tumor was just too low in my rectum and in a place that could not be salvaged or repaired. After this daunting news, I pushed to know the rest of the plan. The regimen would include this surgery, plus chemotherapy and radiation. Such a tough regimen, he informed us, would require an extreme time for recovery after a formidable and lengthy term of treatment.

I decided it was time to call my Thursday morning buddies who had convinced me to get a colonoscopy! This was the beginning of a prayer chain that has supported me to this day. They began to pray in earnest for my situation. My pastor asked if he could announce it at the church to have the people pray, to which I gave my full blessing. Our church congregation was already also praying for my good friend and a co-pastor, Rick Berlin, who had also been diagnosed with cancer, multiple myeloma. His diagnosis was a few months prior to mine, so this became quite an issue with our church, two of our pastoral staff members now having been given a diagnosis of cancer, both with bleak prognoses.

Consequently the church began to pray, and much to my surprise, thousands of people have prayed and continue to pray for complete healing in our bodies, for both Rick and myself. That was one of the most important things to me, to get those prayer warriors going, to get people praying and let God have His way here.

I'll say more about the Miracle of Prayer in a later chapter, but for now, this is what I told the surgeon. We are going to pray. We will do everything we know to do and let God decide what He's going to do.

Soon Dr. Bob introduced us to the final member of our original medical team, my Radiation Oncologist. This doctor immediately ordered a PET scan from which he determined I had a "regional" tumor along with two lymph nodes which were communicating with the tumor. We considered this to be good news since the tumor was regionalized and the PET scan did not indicate a cancer up-take anywhere else in my body. In other words, nothing else lit up! Susan and I were relatively pleased with that information because we knew we were only going to have to work in that pelvic area. Now, we knew what we were going to have to do and thought it would be treatable to a degree. We knew we were going to have surgery, followed by adjuvant and neo-adjuvant chemotherapy, before and after my radiation treatments. We also knew I would lose my rectum and live with a colostomy bag.

As a final note on the Miracle of Diagnosis, my cancer by definition was Stage 3. "Staging" for my type of tumor, in layman's terms, is like this: If the tumor is small inside the colon or rectal wall, it can be a Stage 1. If the tumor gets into but not through the rectal wall, it is considered Stage 2. If it gets into or through the rectal wall and involves less than 4 lymph nodes, it is a Stage 3. If it goes through the rectal wall and involves 4 lymph nodes and is in another organ, it is considered Stage 4.

Stage 4 is where my cancer would ultimately land. For that part of the story, we will turn to a later chapter, but for now, Susan and I were comfortable with the diagnosis and its degree of treatability. We were especially pleased with our team. We felt prepared and at peace to begin the process.

CHAPTER 2

OUR JOURNEY BEGINS

by Susan Tuberville

The journey we walk changes daily, and truly I am grateful for that! How boring life would be if we had no curves in the road. But sometimes the turns our lives take set us back, demanding us to reevaluate EVERYTHING we thought we knew about life.

That's what happened to our journey in September of 2012.

I refer to this as 'Our Journey' and you may have noticed Durell uses the term 'we' oftentimes when telling his story. Let me try to give some perspective to this paradigm. Durell and I met when we were only twelve years old; there is only one month's difference in our ages. We met at church the summer before we would both begin eighth grade. Today, thirty-seven plus years later, we are fifty-five years old. So, suffice it to say, to me life is hard to imagine without Durell. He has been my partner, pastor, friend, lover, and provider for many more years than he was not.

I will try to avoid restating facts that have already been laid out in this account, but I'm sure there will be some redundancy as I tell this tale from my side. Please bear with me.

Durell's first colonoscopy was routine, or so we thought. Our news was pretty run-of-the-mill at that visit: a few polyps, some major hemorrhoids but nothing to worry too much about. However, a plan was made to help with hemorrhoid pain.

The hemorrhoid pain, Durell attributed in part to getting older. Of course at fifty-four years of age, we were seeing daily the changes that aging brings. As my father used to say, "Getting old ain't for sissies." Durell had recently spent one weekend, flat on his back from pain, which we thought was from picking up pecan limbs on the property. After a visit to a chiropractor and many soaks in a hot bath, with Advil and anti-inflammatory cream, he was pretty much back to his regular routine. During this time, he had also developed lots of problems with urination. Again he was quick to attribute these symptoms to common middle-aged men complaints. He talked about seeing a urologist, but the timing wasn't good; after all, he was trying to address a hemorrhoid issue and had just lost precious time to that back strain. He would eventually "get around to it." All of these pains and episodes, I now believe to have been many warning signs. There were many issues we did not initially see as related; however, I think in hindsight they very well may have been.

As Durell's ability to empty his bladder began to be a bigger issue than the hemorrhoids, he eventually scheduled an appointment with his urologist. That's when the discovery of a mass during the digital exam caused the urologist to send Durell straight back to the gastrointestinal team for a lower sigmoid colonoscopy.

This time, we didn't see the procedure as merely routine, and afterward, the doctor told him he had indeed found and biopsied a mass. At this news, Durell was (for Durell) overly distraught. Naturally, the doctor tried to reassure Durell that the results were not in yet and that he would get back with him as soon as he knew anything.

Durell's uncharacteristically troubled reaction, although I'm sure may have had a lot to do with coming out from under the anesthesia, was as telling to me as the urologist's earlier findings. I'm not really sure Durell was even aware of his own uneasy manner, but for me, it was as if all the other tell-tale signs and symptoms were coming together to form a picture neither of us wanted to see. Something much bigger than hemorrhoids, low urine flow, or old age had suddenly interrupted our journey.

On Wednesday, September 28, Durell received the phone call from his gastrointestinal doctor and soon afterward called me with the news. Yes, I said "called me." I was at work, too. I stepped away from my desk and walked to an area where I could have a little more privacy, as the questions were beginning to flood my mind. However, at the time, I could not even formulate them. I don't remember a lot about the phone conversation mostly that he did not sound overly upset. He was very matter-of-fact, repeating I'm sure the same phrases he had heard from the doctor just minutes before. What I do remember is that he wanted to consult Dr. Bob, an oncologist whom we knew we could trust.

The G.I. offices had already set Durell an appointment time with a colorectal surgeon whom we would be seeing later that week.

That evening we processed the information together, first in the kitchen and later on the front porch. The one thing we knew without a doubt was we would get through this together! AND we also knew God would be with us on the journey. It is my chosen belief that God is GOOD and that He is the same yesterday, today, and forever. He will not leave us or forsake us.

As I said, our appointment had been set with the colorectal surgeon. On that day, we were ushered into the exam room where the doctor briefed us on what his role would be. After the exam, he told us as a matter of fact, "Yes, the tumor's placement would require a permanent colostomy." He would have to take out all the potentially compromised tissue in the immediate area of the tumor. There was no "we'll see if we can do something different." He was just as definite as he could be. He informed us that this would require radiation and chemotherapy before and after this major surgery. . . . I knew immediately I wanted a second opinion.

Even though these procedures are everyday procedures to these doctors, they are life-altering procedures to the patient. I wanted to pursue other opinions. As a matter of fact, as soon as the doctor stepped out of the room, I was on the phone asking a friend of mine to call another surgeon, one in whom we—Durell and I both—had great confidence, to see if he performed colorectal surgeries. I told Durell about my trepidation concerning a decision so quickly made, based only on this one opinion, and he reassured me that we would do our research before scheduling anything.

Again, we shored each other up with the promises of God. We were both holding on with a death grip to promises like, "He will never leave us or forsake us" and "Cast all your care on him, for he cares for you."

We quickly conducted as much research as possible, finding online information about this particular diagnosis, as well as consulting with persons whose opinions we respect in the medical field. Upon our first visit with Dr. Bob, he too reassured us that he had confidence in the colorectal surgeon and that the surgeon's professional opinion, to take all the surrounding tissue with the tumor, was the only sound option. After learning all we could, we buckled our seat belts and got ready for the ride.

Durell talked to a lot of people, all of whom began praying for him (for us). One dear friend, John Fulco, had a relative who had been through a similar situation. She had used the same medical team and had a colostomy, although hers was reversible. John asked Durell if he would like to talk to her about her experience, to hear exactly what lay ahead. She was about a year and a half into her post-surgery journey and was getting her life back. When Durell called her, he put her on speaker phone so I could hear the details first hand.

She was very generous with her story. Her experience with the chemo, radiation and surgery opened my eyes, and for the first time, I did not view all this in theoretical possibilities but as reality. My spirits dropped as I began to see the reality of the changes which were in store. I did not like what I was hearing.

It is a fact that opposites attract. I know we have all heard this with a limited understanding of how and why it works. However, to say that Durell and I are opposites is an understatement. We do share many values and beliefs, even lots of interests and activities. But, my personality is mired in realism, fact, and proof. Durrell's, I often say, is the "happy go lucky" style or the "floating along in the clouds," "flying by the seat of your pants" style. Do the terms introvert and extrovert ring any bells here? This man is "social" personified. He is bubbly and boisterous and, yes, opinionated. He is compassionate and gregarious. . . . Getting the picture here? I, on the other hand, want all available information and would also like to see all the particular outcome possibilities when faced with a decision. Therefore, my input is more often than not less than welcome, as it is viewed as the naysayer's, or the Negative Nelly's, viewpoint. However, this disparity of personality between us does, somehow, balance us, and fortunately our balancing scale hasn't often tipped too far off center.

So we listened to the description of how the chemo treatments affected this lady and how she worked through it. She began to explain how neuropathy had developed in her hands and feet, the difficulty she was overcoming just to walk, the struggle she still has with writing or even holding a pencil, and the fact that she could no longer knit because she could not feel the needles or the pressure it took to complete a stitch.

I began to withdraw. I was subconsciously counting off all the things Durell enjoyed which now he would surely lose. All the many things that bring him pleasure, like riding motorcycles, ball room dancing lessons (yes, he truly enjoyed those), hunting, fishing, and wrestling with five grandsons... The list went on and on.

Durell had already adopted an attitude about how he would manage himself through this process, and the last thing I wanted was to bring the "negative" side to every conversation, so I internalized my fears. I began a grieving process that lasted several months. I continued to pray and believe that God was here for us, that He would not put more on us than we could bear, that He was the friend who sticks closer than a brother. Most of all, I continued to believe and claim that God is and always will be GOOD! These facts (and for us they are truly facts), however, did not dissuade me from grieving for all the joys I thought would be lost to Durell (to us) by walking through this journey.

CHAPTER 3

THE MIRACLE OF M.D. ANDERSON

A round this time, I received a call from my oldest son, Josh, who was 33 at the time. He said, "Daddy, Claleigh and I are praying for you, and believing for a healing as said in the Word, but I just keep getting this feeling in my gut, that you should go to M.D. Anderson."

I said, "Ok, I'll take that into consideration."

I had no intentions of going to M.D. Anderson. I had complete confidence in my team here. I had already called some of my physician friends here and had received great reviews regarding my current team. I was very satisfied. My objectives did not include M.D. Anderson, Baylor or anywhere else.

Then my friend Mark Connella called me. Mark is part of my Thursday morning Men's group. We have been friends since high school. He is a member of my board of directors at Personal Solutions, my counseling and psychology company. He and I have travelled extensively together, regionally and nationally. Together, we have responded to Crisis situations, including the Oklahoma City Bombing in 1994. We have taught Critical Incident Stress Management (CISM) together for years. So Mark called me . . . "Hey man, I just have this feeling in my gut that you need to go to M.D. Anderson." Mind you, this call from Mark came the day after Josh's call.

Would you believe I kind of blew Mark off? I said," Well, I appreciate it; I love you, but I think I will stay here!" I did commit to think about it. But I really did not want to go to M.D. Anderson!

Thursday rolls around that very same week, and we have our regular men's group meeting at 6:30am. After the meeting that morning, my longtime friend of 25 years, David Glass, sort of drags around, not wanting to leave. It might interest you to know that David himself is a cancer survivor. He had Waldenstroms cancer. Susan and I are very close to him and his wife Paula, so when David was having treatment a few years back, we wanted to support them through their battle. We even drove to M.D. Anderson just to sit with Paula during one of David's treatments. So . . . this particular morning, David is lollygagging around after our men's meeting, standing on the front porch of my office, when finally, he says, "Bud, I'm not trying to get in your business, and I don't want you to think just because I had cancer, I know everything about cancer, but I really think you need to go to M.D. Anderson and let them look at you."

By now, I am starting to think about it. Maybe God is trying to say something here. As the Bible says, "Out of the mouth of two or three witnesses, let every word be established. . ." Well, Sunday came, and my Pastor, Denny Duron, pulled me aside prior to church service to say, "I have been praying about this thing, and I think you should go to M.D. Anderson." I said, "Well, I have been thinking a lot about that and been praying about it. I'm happy with my team here." He replied without hesitation: "Don't think about it anymore. Just go!"

Here was the fourth person within a week who told me the same thing!! God was obviously saying something, but I am very hard-headed at times.

That same day after church, two friends briskly approached me. It's normal for Mike Pitman and Marshall Jones to banter small talk with me a bit, but this day, they seemed to have a bigger purpose in mind. First, Mike says, "We have something to say to you. . . Marshall called me Saturday night and said, 'I've been praying for Durell, and something keeps saying, "M.D. Anderson!" But I really don't know how to tell Durell'."

I'm steady listening to their story while Mike continues: "Then, I said to Marshall, 'I've been getting the same thing when I pray! And I know exactly how to tell Durell—We will just go up to him and tell him!'" So that's what they did! Of course, I replied, "Funny you should say that." Then I recounted to them the story of the past week.

Now, finally, I was convinced! Ready to acquiesce, I told the Lord I was sorry for not listening, and I repented for my stubbornness. The next day, Monday morning, I called Dr. Bob to tell him I thought I needed to go to M.D. Anderson. He sighed on the other end of the line, saying "I am so glad you told me that. I was praying for you this weekend, and I felt like you should go to M.D. Anderson."

So now, a total of 7 people in one week had told me the same exact message. I asked Dr. Bob if he could make it happen, to which he happily replied, "Absolutely." His office had me an appointment for less than two weeks away, which is nothing short of amazing to get in that quickly. Putting all that together, I deduced that the Lord must have a reason for us to go to M.D. Anderson (I was yet to fully relinquish my hardheadedness).

Something I have failed to mention about this week is that it was a particularly tough time for me on a different personal level. My mom had been battling a form of ALS for a little over ten years, and now she was dealing with end-of-life issues. Inside of me, there was a lot going on. My mother had been such a special person to me all of my life. If you pick up the dictionary and look up Southern Belle, her picture would be there beside it. A Southern Belle, indeed, and one who loved God—heart, soul, mind and body. She always embodied the faith I aspired to live. Even after wrestling ALS for so many drawn out years, she never lost her faith. She never even lost her smile, and she never lost her desire to encourage others. From the time she was diagnosed until she could no longer draw a breath, she was an inspiration to all who came to see her. She really taught me how to deal with difficult physical situations. She loved to be involved with people, her family, children, grandchildren, great-grandchildren, and her church family. She loved to cook. She was a biscuit making machine. Even with the harsh diagnosis of debilitating ALS, she ran forward with all her energy.

When my diagnosis was handed down, she was beginning her closing physical days. On that September morning 2012, when I told her about my diagnosis, she could hardly make a sound, much less talk. All she could do was reach over and pat me on the hand. I knew she understood. In her spirit and heart, she was there. We never got to talk about my cancer or my treatment process; we were not afforded the pleasure of conversing. After I told her of my prognosis, from then on, I just wanted to focus on her and how I could continue to help her final days be as good as possible. My M.D. Anderson appointment was scheduled for the Monday after Thanksgiving. Mom passed away the Monday before Thanksgiving, November 19, 2012. She was buried the day after Thanksgiving, just two days before I was to head to whatever awaited me at M.D. Anderson.

I know coming from a guy who was fifty-four years old at the time, it sounds odd to say that I needed my mom, but . . . I really needed my mom. Don't get me wrong, I did have incredible support around me, but there was something about the role she had always played in my life, and at this point, I still wanted her in that role. She was the one whom I always bounced things off of. She was the rock of our family, but now she would not be there to hear what I was going through. Now, I would not have her support in a tangible way. She taught me so much about living and dying. She taught me to face it with so much grace, so much steadfastness, that no matter what stage I was in, I should be happy and content. I praise the Lord for her and her life and all she taught me. There are many days I think about her and talk to the air as if she were present because I just want to say "Thank You" to her, to tell her I am going to do this! I am going to live the legacy she left me. Mom, I'm not going to let you down! I'm not going to fuss and complain about this diagnosis, about my treatments, about not feeling good.

She never said a word about her pain, discomfort, or any negative thing she was going through. I lean on that quite a bit, even today. I want that to be a part of me. When I get to heaven, if it matters, I want to hear God say, "Well done, thou good and faithful servant," and I want to hear my mom say, "I'm proud of you."

The Sunday after we buried Mom, we headed for M.D. Anderson. Susan and I thought it would be good for my Dad to accompany us so he could hear the word about my cancer straight from the horse's mouth, whatever that word was going to be. Dad and Mom had purchased a very nice handicap van to accommodate her needs with ALS, so Dad offered to drive us to down to Houston in real comfort.

Upon arrival, I made sure the colorectal surgeon at M.D. Anderson was aware of my objective—to confirm the diagnosis we had received in Shreveport and get some verification through a second opinion. Being a man of few words, the surgeon performed a thorough initial exam and sent us straight over for an MRI and CT scan. We were to wait out the rest of the evening and return to hear the results in the morning.

In the morning, a surgical oncologist was waiting to talk to us: "The tests confirmed that there is indeed a rectal adenocarcinoma, but that is not my main concern." That's not what I came to hear, but that's what he was saying. He went on to discuss the main concern. The tests had revealed metastatic disease in the lungs!

Remember the layman's definitions I mentioned before, about the stages of cancer? This new information placed my diagnosis at Stage Four. In one moment, we went from a regionalized stage three tumor to a full-blown Stage Four cancer having spread from my pelvic area to my lungs! All of a sudden, we were hearing a doctor say that surgery for the rectal tumor was not an option. All of a sudden, we were dealing with rectal cancer in my lungs! This realization hit us pretty heavy. Now, we were facing the Big "C."

After giving us the news, this oncologist just walked out.

We sat and looked at each other with empty eyes and stunned emotions. We cried and hugged without knowing what to say or do. The deer-in-the-head-lights look followed by more crying, again and again, we were overwhelmed. When the doctor returned, he was very matter of fact. Because of the metastasis in the lungs, the previously agreed upon plan for rectal surgery was no longer an option. Four nodules in the lungs were far too likely to be cancer. With treatment of these nodules, the best prognosis of life expectancy he could offer us was about two years!

A couple hours later, we were in the office of a research oncologist, a delightful young doctor who was ready to answer all our questions and help us navigate this new prognosis. Susan asked one question which had been of great concern to us both: Is this type of cancer something I could pass on to my boys? The mother in Susan immediately went to those two young men, who now have boys of their own. The doctor actually had to do quite a bit of further testing to determine this answer, but at the end of the week, his report indicated my cancer is not hereditary but rather environmental. Such comforting news was quite welcome, to know that my boys, and their boys, were not at risk of facing this same diagnosis one day.

We also asked him all about the prognosis and potential treatment modalities. He recommended chemotherapy—a FOLFOX Cocktail—which is a mixture of 5-FU (Fluorouracil), Avastin and Oxaliplatin. We talked extensively about the four identifiable nodules in my lungs. They were very small, the largest falling between 8 and 9 millimeters, which is about the size of an eraser on a #2 pencil. I also wanted to know—since we were talking about infusing this cocktail into my whole body—how we could be sure the nodules were actually cancer. "We are not 100 percent sure," he replied, "but with all the other markers in your body, with the rectal adenocarcinoma, and the identified

lymph nodes, we are pretty sure this is cancer in these nodules."
Wow! "But what if it's not?" I asked. He reiterated, "With all the
other markers, I would treat it the same." He explained that the
only way to find out would be to do a lung biopsy, either opening
up the chest and taking a sample, or sticking a needle into my
lungs to snip a piece from the nodules. "Ok," I remarked and
continued, "If you do a needle biopsy and find out that it is the
same cancer, the rectal adenocarcinoma, do you treat it the same
way?" He said, "Yes." "So, if you don't know or you do know,
you still recommend treatment the same way?" He again
concurred. From the sound of it, I was entering into a new world
of FOLFOX Infusion Therapy.

Next, I asked if I could do the treatment in Shreveport.
Although they really wanted me to do it in Houston, I could think
of many reasons not to drive back and forth from Shreveport,
Louisiana to Houston, Texas every other week for who knows
how long. They're telling me I only have two years to live, even
with this chemo cocktail therapy, so I don't think I really want to
spend that much time on the road between home and the
hospital. The ultimate conclusion would come after M.D.
Anderson's research oncologist and Dr. Bob had time to consult
and concur with each other on the mode of treatment. My request
for Dr. Bob at this point was to be able to administer my
treatments in Shreveport, and he assured me that we could in
conjunction with the oncologist in Houston.

After meeting with the physicians at M.D. Anderson, Susan
and I told Dad the outcome, and we all headed home, but I asked
Dad if he would mind if I drove home. I only wanted to focus on
driving and not have to talk. Consequently, the next four hours
were relatively quiet as we drove from Houston to Shreveport.

Two years to live.

I just heard from the best medical opinions we could get.
From M.D. Anderson's Surgical and Research Oncology
departments, to Schumpert Cancer Treatment Center's Dr. Bob,
to Willis Knighton's colorectal surgeon, to my G.I. Doctor and my

Urologist, all confirmed the cancer was there. Six doctors all could see it. They had digitally felt it. They had traced it with the MRI, CAT scan, and Pet scans. And I was about to live it. That's what I had to think about on our drive home. Driving would give me the time to consider how I wanted to live these last two years. During that ride home, I worked very hard at getting my game face on. It had to last until either I died or was miraculously healed.

So we came home resolved that I had two years to live, plus or minus a few months. However, we also resolved that God is able to do anything! Our faith was in God. We were going to pray for complete healing, and that is exactly what we began to do! We again enlisted the power of prayer, through prayer warriors. We also began exercising our faith. Yes, we would follow the medical treatment which had been set before us, but ultimately God is the healer. That was the only way I could see myself managing this process. To my knowledge I had not caused this disease. I had no control over its establishment in my body, and I could only do as I was told in addressing its treatment. I found myself completely at the mercy of physicians and in the hand of God. It is the "in the hand of God" part that I was going to focus on. The Miracle of M.D. Anderson had proven we were in His hands.

As Uncle Remus said in his story *Brer Rabbit Visits de Witch Rabbit*, I, given the circumstances, could live in "de mopes." But just like Aunt Mammy-Bammy Big-Money showed Brer Rabbit, the things God has already given me would last for eternity, and so there went "the mopes."

Game On!

CHAPTER 4

M.D. ANDERSON

by Susan Tuberville

Somewhere along about this time, Durell began to receive counsel from others about pursuing a second opinion at M.D. Anderson instead of just accepting the fact that he would have a permanent colostomy. We consulted his oncologist, and he agreed that, were he in Durell's situation, he too would want to check out all available resources. At that point they scheduled us an appointment, and we took off for a week's worth of tests in Houston. In my mind, this was all about checking out any advances in treatment, a robotic surgery perhaps that might save the sphincter muscle, or some other such advance which Shreveport had yet to adopt.

We began with a meeting with the surgeon at M.D. Anderson where he did his own thorough exam of Durell's tumor. He quickly concurred that with the location of the tumor, the only option would be to remove the anus and sphincter muscles as our colorectal surgeon had already determined. He would be happy to do the surgery, but concurred with the standard procedure offered at Shreveport which meant radiation and chemo before and after surgery. There was no real difference in what was offered, but we at least felt we had checked out our options.

We left that appointment to go back to the hotel room and shore ourselves up for the future. We googled "colostomy" one hundred different ways and found that people with colostomies can adjust and live relatively normal lifestyles. We also found out that oftentimes, no one even knows you have a colostomy. People with colostomies are often still athletically active and often return to their normal routines without much change to everyday life. We looked at the different styles and terms so we could more intelligently discuss these options with the doctor upon our return visit. Again, I like lots of information. We discussed the different appliances, bags, etc. that would all become part of our new lifestyle. We also determined if the same standard was to be followed as had been laid out for us in Shreveport, we would prefer to have it all done in Shreveport. Again, Durell was confident with his team, and to us it just made more sense to be at home. This was the decision we made that night at our hotel, and we had prepared to thank the doctor for his opinion and continue this journey at home where it had begun.

In the meantime, we spent the next few days with Durell undergoing a battery of tests and scans. We were prepared to head back to Shreveport after our follow up appointment with the surgeon once he had evaluated the radiologists' reports and discussed what was next.

That next appointment was a game changer. The surgical oncologist and his assistant entered the room and began to talk about what the scans showed for the tumor. It had grown through the rectal wall and was placing pressure on the prostate. They said it may even be communicating with the spleen. He added that there were several lymph nodes involved and, most disturbing, several bilateral lung nodules were found consistent with progression of metastatic disease with significant evidence of vascular invasion.

I'm sure our faces were blank, with questions evidenced though yet unvoiced. How quickly I forgot all my concerns regarding the best type appliance for fitting Durell's colostomy to his activity level! I seemed to forget everything, except the words "metastatic disease." In the past month, although I had not become an expert, I had read A LOT of information online regarding colorectal cancer and staging. The prognosis for stage 3 colorectal cancer was challenging and sobering. The prognosis for stage 4 was terminal. The doctor proceeded to say he hesitated bringing this information to us without the radiologist there to defend it, but that particular radiologist who wrote the report was out for a few days. He did contact another to read the reports before he met with us, and although there was some room for interpretation, both had found there to be metastatic disease in the lungs. He pretty much left the room after he read the report, leaving his assistant behind. She looked at us both and offered heartfelt apologies for what they had to report. She said she would give us some time, as obviously this was not the information any of us were expecting.

I've never witnessed much trauma, but I think I know a little of what victims of shell shock experience. It felt as if we had entered a netherworld, where life was on an altered trajectory. For what seemed like several minutes neither of us could speak; we just held each other. Eventually the doctor came back to the room, and I believe Durell asked a question about the surgery. That is when the surgeon stopped him, looked at us both and said, "There will not need to be a surgery."

He later went on to say people with metastatic disease don't undergo these types of major surgeries. When the cancer has already progressed to other organs, there is no point putting them through it. I did pipe up at this point and ask, "So what is his prognosis?" "Two—two and a half years with medical intervention" was his reply. He told us he had scheduled Durell an appointment with the research oncologist down the hall to discuss a treatment plan. We went to that appointment still in a semi state of shock. This nice young research oncologist began to discuss treatment options.

I remember Durell kept referring to and asking questions about "after the surgery." The doctor, having read Durell's bio from his chart, understood he was speaking to a well-educated man, a man with a doctorate no less, but Durell did not seem to comprehend what the doctor was telling him. I remember him looking searchingly into Durell's face and saying, "You do understand there is no reason to do surgery at this point, right?" Again there was some statement made from Durell, about after the surgery . . . . The doctor conceded the idea but made it plain, the only surgery that might be in store would be a palliative procedure if the rectal tumor continued to grow and closed off the colon to evacuation.

We left that appointment the doctor still puzzled, asking, "You do understand what I've told you, do you not?" Durell's answer rings in my ears today as it did that day, "I believe in you doctor, but I believe more in what He says" and pointed upward. There was no question but that this man, this educated man, placed more trust and faith in what God had in store than what medicine could do.

WOW! God must have more faith in me than I have in myself, if I truly believe he will not put more on us than we can bear. I could only think I really don't know how to bear this. I continued to pray and mine and Durell's conversations changed. I was not sure what to call what I was feeling: doubt, lack of faith, or unbelief. The medical diagnosis and the information I read were warring with my spirit. My prayer had changed; I began to pray as the boy's father did in the book of Mark, "Lord, I believe, help thou my unbelief!" Durell left that appointment with his own version of what was ahead, and I left with a notebook full of radiologists' reports, doctors' opinions, and a future I could no longer see. As we walked out, his dad was there. He had accompanied us on this first trip. I knew I could not answer questions; after all, I didn't have all the information I needed. So, I was quiet as Durell answered his dad's question, "Well, how did it go?" Durell began, "Well, the good news is..." From there,

I can't really tell you what was said. I just know for every phone call he made to family and friends waiting at home for the report, they all began with "The good news is…"

This man of mine, this man of faith, this man with his happy-go-lucky attitude—he at once infuriated me and encouraged me. How can I even express the conflicted emotions that were warring inside me? Part of me wanted to shake him, to read the report to him again, to ask the same questions the doctor had asked, "Are you sure you understand what I'm saying?" But the other part of me rejoiced that he could find this pathway where he could keep his head up, keep his focus, keep his faith and keep being the man God created him to be. He encouraged everyone who called to check on him. He would ask about their wellbeing and their families. Then when they turned the conversation to him, he began, "Well, the good news is…"

I found myself in the back of the van, feigning sleep so I would not have to respond to any conversation that might come my way, praying again and again and again. As Durell made his calls to give information to others, I determined if this is what it takes for him to get through this, I can go along. Only I couldn't, not completely.

In the back of the van, I found myself making whispered phone calls to our sons after they had received the reports from their dad. He did not exactly lie to the boys, but he did not exactly present the information the way it had been presented to us, either. I remember making my decision that our sons should have the complete picture, not just the one presented through dad's rose-colored glasses (Negative Nelly rises again). I, in turn, called each of them and read them the reports the doctor had given. I think not only did I want to make sure the boys were not in the dark, but I also knew I needed their support. My decision to go along with Durell's version of things was about **not** sabotaging his faith, his attitude, and his strategy to beat this, because Lord knows I wanted him to beat it!

During my inner battles with fact and faith, I realized that I did indeed have a fact I could use as my foundation through this battle as well. I had spent way too much time in grief already. I would not grieve my way through this journey; I would wait and grieve when **and if** the time came for grief. For now, we are both very much alive and we will celebrate life!

I also had to admit my selfishness to God. No matter how much I loved this man, I know that God loves him more. So, I came back to our initial consensus reached when we first received his diagnosis—"God is not going to leave us. He may decide to heal Durell and use his testimony for His glory, or He may decide to use the testimony of the journey for His glory, either way God is GOOD and God is with us!"

Chapter 5

The Miracle of Treatment

Before our first trip to M.D. Anderson, we had begun a treatment regimen for the rectal tumor. The initial game plan, beginning with an oral chemotherapy called Xeloda and followed up with a six week regimen of radiation on the tumor site, as you may recall, would finally include surgery to remove the tumor and a significant, permanent portion of the rectum and anus. That procedure, which would have fallen in December 2012, was to leave me with a colostomy.

Susan and I came home from M.D. Anderson to have a Subclavian Porta catheter put in because now we were fighting Stage 4 instead of Stage 3 cancer. The porta-cath surgeon did a great job making this as pleasant an experience as it could be. Since this procedure only required a local anesthesia and a Valium, I was not completely out of it. The doctor and I talked LSU football, while he installed my new equipment. "You have really tough skin!" was an unexpected comment, to which I just had to ask, "Is that a good thing or a bad thing?" Thankfully, that was a good thing; he said tough skin was good for holding these things in place. Then he continued, "Oh, We've got a good back flow here," as he kept things light and made this as fun as possible. He did make it fun, although I would not recommend the procedure to everyone. Afterward, once he was sure things were right, he turned the monitor around so I could see this thing going straight into the arteries in my chest!

Now it was time for Susan and me to meet with Dr. Bob to map out our infusion FOLFOX6 treatment. I have to note here, before we move into the more miserable moments of this journey, that Dr. Bob and his staff were very comforting and thorough, letting us know what to expect. Our nurse, Rene, explained all the possible side effects of the chemotherapy infusion, and then they sent us to attend a class regarding the intricate details. The enormous list of possible side effects, coupled with the prognosis itself, left me and Susan little doubt that I would probably die! It was looking like a sure thing that either the side effects of the chemo and radiation or the cancer itself was going to take me out!

In October, before the Stage 4 diagnosis, I had begun radiation treatments every day at noon. This was ongoing for six weeks. The reason we had radiation at noon was so I could put in some good work at the office before heading to the hospital for treatment. I am a Licensed Professional Counselor, Licensed Marriage and Family Therapist, Chaplain for the Caddo Parish Sheriff's Office, Counselor for Shreveport Community Church, and have several other business endeavors, including—at the time—a restaurant startup my son Dustin and I had just embarked upon in Texarkana, Texas. Keeping up wasn't so bad at first, but as the weeks progressed, things became uncomfortable and more and more painful.

I kept this up for a while, but when fatigue and extreme discomfort began to hinder my effectiveness at work, the emotional and psychological challenges commenced. Growing up with a blue-collar, git-'er-done, work ethic, I had not been prepared for how to respond as work threatened to become almost impossible. Now, with trouble sleeping at night and needing naps in the middle of the day (I had never done "naps" except for the occasional Sunday nap between church services), my schedule was becoming a mess. I did hold it together as long as I could, but it slipped away without my control.

At the same time, another serious challenge was encroaching: a bone-chilling change in my daily bowel routine. The further along I progressed with the radiation, the more and more painful my bowel movements became. Suddenly, I found this basic part of life becoming a dramatic challenge. I tried to avoid eating anything of real consistency because elimination was excruciating! Sweating profusely and shaking from the pain, I would have to bite down on a rolled-up wash cloth in order to keep from screaming out. What I would call an unbearable circumstance was now something I had to bear every day.

And that was not the whole story with my bowels because, as we had been warned, new issues continued to surface. These are the kinds of issues all the warnings in the world do not prepare you for; nobody grows up being taught how to deal with this. You see, in addition to the horrible pain of a regular bowel movement, this chemotherapy regimen began to result in extreme diarrhea. The agitation of uncontrollable diarrhea posed an awful mental challenge to me: here I am in my mid-fifties, and if I need to leave my house, I have to wear a diaper and take a backpack full of emergency supplies. When my children were infants, diapers and emergency bags were normal, but now? This was terrible. My morning routine, because of my bathroom needs, became a process of hours. This country boy was used to getting ready quick and getting straight to where he needed to be, but now, just going to work or church was a major endeavor.

Then, in mid-December of 2012, when the Stage 4 fight was full-on FOLFOX Chemotherapy administered via ambulatory pump for a period of 72 hours every 2 weeks—the most aggressive treatment possible to address my situation, yet still with a two-year life expectancy, the drain on my energy and schedule went beyond anything I had imagined. Every other week on Tuesday, Susan would drive me to the Schumpert Cancer Center. There I would receive five to six hours of treatment, only to be released home with a fanny pack pump pushing more meds into my Porta Cath for the next 46 hours. Thursday afternoon, we would return to have the pump removed. Our plan called for 12 rounds in this bout, lasting 24 weeks, that is, if everything worked without complication.

My personality is rather aggressive, so the time spent resting on my laurels as this medicine made its way into my body was miserable, to say the least. Doing nothing and missing out on life was not a concept I could be happy about. As much as the doctor had talked about the drain on my energy and possible ramifications of what I was about to go through, I was completely ignorant of how this was going to affect me. I didn't know what "rest" meant, but I was having rest forced upon me. Well, "rest" might be the wrong word because I did not really rest. . . . My chemotherapy cocktail assaulted me with perpetual nausea. During the entire treatment, for four and five days at a time, I always felt just a few minutes away from throwing up. A blessing to note is that I have never actually thrown up during this whole time; nevertheless, the incessant need to vomit never left me.

Along with losing my calm stomach, I was also losing the things I enjoyed most in life, like duck hunting or riding my motorcycle. These were things that had always rejuvenated me and relieved my stress, but now I was having to say "no" every time a friend would mention doing something like this together. However, my friends are such great friends that they stepped to the plate with other ways for us to spend time together. I will detail more about the Miracle of Friendship in a later chapter, but for now, suffice it to say, as difficult as it might seem to other personality types, for me, having friends around regenerates me and helps me find the real rest I needed. To go through all these losses and pains, my spirit surely would have been broken without the help of my friends.

One friend I will mention now, because he helped me discover another miserable side effect of Oxaliplatin. When we had just started the cocktail treatment, we were a little apprehensive for me to stay home alone before we knew how my body was going to react, and since Susan works part time as a school counselor, we asked a retired firefighter friend of mine, Buddy Parker, to hang out with me on one of those first days. Buddy laughed at the idea of babysitting me, but he nevertheless agreed to. Buddy didn't just babysit me, however. Instead, he took me out on the town for some errands and some Chic-Fil-A, where I ordered an ice-cold chocolate milkshake to go with my chicken and waffle fries. Now, since you might not know me very well, I'll go ahead and tell you. . . I love ice cream. I love milkshakes, root beer floats, or anything that involves ice cream. Spoiler alert: if you share my love for ice cream, you might want to skip over the next side effect because it is just too depressing.

Buddy and I were eating and talking, and everything was going fine until I took that first drink of milkshake. As it ran down my throat, suddenly I felt as if I had swallowed broken concrete, cutting and tearing its way down to my stomach. "There is something in this milkshake!" was my first response. It never crossed my mind to associate the scratching and pulling of the flesh in my throat with everything else I was going through, so I insisted on finding whatever foreign object in this milkshake could be ripping through my throat. I took the lid off, stirred it around and searched, but since I couldn't find anything, I took another sip. And, dadgum, it hurt again!! I never claimed to be the sharpest knife in the drawer.

Buddy, on the other hand, remembered something we had seen that morning while we were glancing through the drug paperwork. He recognized what was going on: "It's the cold!" I was still a little dumbfounded until he explained further that hypersensitivity to cold was one of the side effects of Oxaliplatin. Of course, I immediately quit drinking the milkshake. Instead, we had a great laugh when I took it home and heated it up in the microwave. I was not going to lose that ice cream even if I had to drink it warm. And drink it I did.

That story was kind of funny, but soon I realized hypersensitivity to cold is no laughing matter. To stand in front of an open refrigerator or to touch a glass of ice tea would now be akin to pin pricks or even electric shock. One of our original panic moments occurred in January 2013. By December and January in the Deep South, it finally gets cold enough for us to grab a coat.

One day that January, the trunk light in Susan's car had gone out so I wrapped up in a coat and hat, and climbed into her trunk to replace the bulb. As I was lying on my back (with my Infusion Pump on in my fanny pack), my body began to respond as if I were in anaphylactic shock. My bronchioles swelled, wheezing set in, and breathing became very difficult. Susan and I both felt panicky, and she even considered calling 911 because my breathing seemed to want to quit altogether, but once we got inside, where it was 75 degrees, my breathing returned to normal. I was happy for the warm house, but from that day on, I learned I needed to keep a hair dryer close by in case I ever breathed too much cold air again. Sure enough, blowing a hair dryer in my face would bring my breathing back to normal pretty quickly. That's good to know when there's no way to avoid cold, wintery air.

I had to wrestle with all these things day-by-day. The hypersensitivity to cold stole my freedom to work outside — or to drink anything worth drinking — and affected me negatively in any activity that required contact with something cooler than 75 degrees . . . like ice cream. At the same time, fatigue was wrecking my work schedule and my ability to serve in the community. As if that wasn't enough, agonizing bowel movements hurt as bad as anything I had ever experienced, nausea was unrelenting, and diarrhea ruined my sheets in the night while assaulting my dignity by day. Finally, I was losing all connection to the things I enjoyed, from piddling in my shop, to riding the country roads on my motorcycle. All this came together to back me into a tight spot.

Intermittently during treatments, the medical professionals would try to assess whether I might be dealing with depression over all this. That sounds like a natural conclusion, but I would always answer, "I don't get depressed." Truly, I didn't get depressed, but I did get confused. I might even get angry — I might just go ahead and hit something — but I wasn't depressed. The way I solve problems is to get quiet and think my way to an answer, but with cancer I couldn't think through to any solutions at all. No processes I had ever learned applied to cancer. I wanted to go on with life as if nothing had changed, but reality was forcing me to manage my body in new ways.

Depression was definitely a viable option, but I also had a lot going for me. Treatment is a real miracle. It was a wonderful blessing to have the treatment team at Christus Cancer Treatment Center. Those nurses are spectacular in how they care for patients. The hospital has several rooms facing northeast with huge window walls filled with mini blinds. I call these the Penthouse suites. I always requested one of those rooms. Soon the nurses would meet Susan and me at the counter and say, "The penthouse is ready for you." My nurses, of whom there were many, were absolutely the best for me. They tolerated the loud laughter and conversations that went on while my friends came to visit during the Tuesday treatment days. The miracle of treatment certainly included these wonderful girls being there week after week during the entire time.

I received chemotherapy infusion treatments through May of 2014.

CHAPTER 6

PHYSICAL TRIALS OF TREATMENT

by Susan Tuberville

There were many months of physical trials which began even before Durell's cancer diagnosis, before his first colonoscopy.

I mentioned the prostate issue early on. This was no little thing for him even though he wanted to think so (After all, wasn't it just the issues of a benign enlarged prostate. Don't all middle aged men have some problem with this?) Durell had major issues voiding. At different times he would have to immerse himself in a warm tub of water just to be able to get his bladder to void completely. He was already taking medication for this but found it was no longer working.

Durell had lower back discomfort and pain. There were times we thought we could trace the pain to some overexertion which might have exacerbated the problem, but other times he just was uncomfortable. We wondered if it was just too much sitting during counseling sessions in the office. Some days ran from 9a.m. until 6p.m. with little other than a bathroom break. This theory for his lingering discomfort seemed the most sensible. The other problem we knew about was his hemorrhoid issues, so we also blamed a lot of his pain on this. Of course, now we realized all these issues may have been tied to the tumor **growing at the junction of his rectum and anus.** For a man who had little history of medical issues these were trying times in and of themselves.

Durell has always been the one to offer help to those in need, so to be "the man in need" was an entirely new concept for him, and for myself as well. I remember a situation in our earliest time of ministry as youth pastors when Durell first showed signs of always wanting to be there for others. He was late for a meeting with the head pastor, who proceeded, naturally, to reprimanded Durell and lecture him on the importance of punctuality. Of course, Durell agreed and apologized, but then he said, "People are more important than punctuality," and he explained to the pastor that on his way to the meeting, he passed one of their parishioners on the side of the road. One of this man's cows had gotten out, so Durell stopped to help him and stayed with him until the animal was back in pasture where it belonged. For Durell, people have always trumped any other need or expectation.

It is my belief that the foundation Durell laid in our lives based on Joshua's declaration "As for me and my house, we will serve the Lord" has also been the foundation from which the blessings and support we have received throughout this journey have come. Part of Durell's philosophy in life is that Jesus meant it when he said, "No greater love has any man than he would lay down his life for a fellow man" (paraphrased). Durell has always believed this and taught that it is not in the dying but in the living that Jesus was admonishing us to lay down our lives for others. To give up your time, your pursuits, and your money for your fellow man—that is to truly love.

The physical challenges of the initial chemo were minimal. Durell seemed to take the oral Xeloda with no problem and no obvious side effects. The radiation, however, was a different story. As it destroyed the tumor, it also caused great pain in Durell's rectum. Sitting became difficult, and as you can imagine, with a job as a counselor, that was no small challenge. We even entertained the idea of a standing desk as we looked at options for comfort. Driving and riding in his rough old truck became a literal pain in the rectum (and lower back). Throughout each stage of treatment, new pains were emerging.

Once we had our diagnosis from M.D. Anderson and he began the infusion chemotherapy, even more challenges arose. Constant negative factors included a depletion of energy and strength with an overall yucky feeling, like coming down with the flu, every day—not to mention, going to the hospital every other week, sitting for 5-7 hours for the chemo administration, and then leaving with an infusion pump still attached (for the next 46 hours) to continue poisoning the cancer cells—along with the healthy cells. These were not just major inconveniences; they were physically debilitating. Also, the steroid administered along with the chemo caused insomnia, while the discomfort of an intravenous pump tied around his waist and connected with an IV to a port in his chest made sleeping almost impossible anyway.

Durell met all these challenges with a fervor that only he could. He would not give in to the discomfort or the despair, like most of us would have. Without fail, to everyone he came in contact with, he continued to express that he was "Living the Miracle." What had once been a point of frustration for me—to hear him extol the "good news" about his condition—had now turned into my saving grace. Had I been married to a man with a "can't do" kind of attitude instead of the "can do" man Durell is, I doubt I could have carried his burden along with my own. As it was, he was determined to **live his miracle**, with no gaps provided for the devil to get a foothold.

CHAPTER 7

THE MIRACLE OF A DREAM

I work part-time on our church staff as a counselor and in several other capacities as the needs demand. I don't remember the date of the following story, but I remember the details verbatim, and I will never forget the impact it had on my life.

I happened one regular weekday to run by our church on a routine matter. I simply needed to drop some paperwork off to Emily, one of our wonderful executive team members. However, when our senior pastor happened to hear my voice from the room where he was, he interrupted his own meeting to step out to see me. That's when my routine visit took a turn toward the miraculous. "I want you to come in here when you finish your business" was all he said, so a few minutes later, I was in his office with the other staff pastors who had been meeting with him. I hoped they would all pardon my interruption as Pastor turned the attention toward me: "I've obviously been praying for you and thinking about what has been going on." Then he added, "I had a vision, a word from the Lord that I want to give you."

When Pastor Denny Duron says that, I listen. I always consider Pastor Denny's opinion and view to be important, but when he says he has a word from the Lord, he means it, and I have grown to appreciate how accurately the Lord speaks to this man's heart. Even though the battle I am presently facing seems completely physical, as a spiritual man, I always want to be in touch with what the Lord is saying in my life. Pastor Denny continued, "I had a dream of you being completely healthy and completely healed. Cancer is not going to take your life. The word of the Lord is that Cancer is not going to take your life!"

Now, that was no small thing to say! Remember, I had just been told by the doctors at M.D. Anderson that even with treatment, the best prognosis I had was two years to live. This is a pretty powerful prophecy, indeed. So I began to think, "Ok, God, you have spoken this through the word of my Pastor, and I am going to hold on to it."

Pastor Denny even added that he had a vision of me being healthy and doing the work of the Lord. Needless to say I was pretty encouraged. Then he continued, "However . . . the Lord showed me something that is important for you to work on. . . . Now is the time for you to get out of living in idolatry."

Idolatry? Idolatry is having something in one's life that is more concerning or of greater focus and value than God.

He explained further that the idolatry was "not that you have a god that you overtly worship greater than God Almighty, but the idolatry in your life is the fact that you have been constantly trying to prove yourself . . . to do things for other people to prove your value. . . . You work hard and do things well for other people. You inspire and promote other people. You try to reach goals . . . to become that valuable person, in order to feel valuable as a person . . . This has become an idol to you."

That was right on. And suddenly, I found myself experiencing the Miracle of a Dream. Listening to and meditating on all he had said about his dream, I realized pretty easily that I do exactly what he was talking about. I like inspiring others, but I also like the emotional gratification I get from it. Even as far back as my high school athletic career, I can remember this pattern in my motivation and behavior. As an athlete, like most young men, I always wanted to be superior. But I remember wanting to perform at such a level that my team couldn't function without me. That might sound condescending toward my team, but I didn't mean it that way; I just always wanted to be a leader. I wanted to be the one who could rally the troops to perform as a team. I wanted the whole team to win, but my personal value was tied to whether I could be the successful leader. That's what was really important to me.

The majority of my adult life has also been wrapped around those types of things. A part of my personality wants to be valued as the "go to" guy. As a dad, I try to provide avenues and opportunities for my boys to succeed better than I did. The same thing is true with my staff at work. I want my staff to know that my role is to help them succeed. This is a great quality in a boss, but to me, my personal value had become locked in to whether or not I succeeded at these things. A lot of what I have done to assist and inspire others was to prove that I was valuable.

Here I was with cancer, unable to "do" anything worthwhile, unable to accomplish any of the things which heretofore had given me value. The cancer treatment was reducing me to a point of need which I had never faced before. My ability to perform as a man, as a husband, as a businessman, as a church leader and as a leader to my office staff was all but gone. The whole year of 2013, my productivity was about 3.5 months. The rest of the time, I was out sick, having treatment, and even in the hospital (during a terribly long episode which we'll discuss in a later chapter). I was being cared for and tended to. I was no longer valuable.

I would even say that a victim mentality was trying to set in. Cancer and disease can work on one's mind; at least it did on mine. My cancer is environmental, not hereditary. If it were hereditary, I might certainly feel like a victim since it would have come from genes which had been passed to me naturally. However, in my mind, even the environmental factor was making me a victim because I had no idea what I had done to cause it. To my knowledge, I could not trace any of my choices to the cause of this cancer—except perhaps my procrastination in getting checked out—so there was no way for me to take the blame (which in a way would make me feel better). Because the doctors can't say, well you did A, B, and C and that is why you got cancer, my thinking was being challenged emotionally and psychologically by the fact that this whole situation was out of my control, making me the victim. A victim mentality can create an obstacle to everything good and productive. The actual battle is against cancer, but with this added sense of being a victim, I couldn't see the battle lines clearly. Again, my value as a man was being eaten away.

Pastor Denny had hit the nail on the head. I had to get to a place where I understood that God values me for who I am more than for what I can produce. Cancer put me in that place. To me, this was a devastating place, but my only hope was to embrace it. I had to grasp this new truth: that my importance to God boiled down to my being Durell Tuberville, not to my being a great producer in His kingdom. From this time on, if I were going to "do" anything, it would have to be because that's just who I am, not because I am trying to prove my value. I began to accept it. . .

With this word from Pastor Denny, I was able to appreciate my value to God just as myself. Ironically, this inspired me to be able to do more! This time, however, I was not "doing" in order to add value to myself in my own eyes. Rather, I would now focus on doing from a different motive. The more that I was able to focus on the things I can do, the less down and depressed I would be. Denny's message that day helped me realize that the way I had been living even before I knew I had cancer was not fully to the glory of God. I had made an idol out of my "works" for God, thinking they made me more valuable to God. I am so grateful for that word from my pastor, who had the courage to reveal his dream to me and speak a difficult truth to me.

If you are dealing with the same sort of feelings, I hope you will accept this miracle and let it encourage you. As my pastor told me, I am telling you, "You have value with God, regardless of what you do, and embracing that is difficult for you." Live or die, your value is in God, not in your ability to beat cancer, not in your ability to perform as a human being so that others can appreciate your performance. God values you because you are you. Embracing God's value of yourself must become your focus. When that happens, your situation—even Stage 4 Colorectal Cancer—cannot be allowed to get you down. Your emotional response to what you are going through will change as you embrace how important you are to God, just for who you are. I know that once you accepted Jesus as Savior, then you began to want to please him with your life. You know the roller-coaster ride of successes and failures, of temptations, trials and tribulations. However, you cannot confuse your desire to please Him with whether or not He loves and adores you. Regardless of whether you or not you "win" your battles, He values you and is for you!

He gave me an opportunity to refocus my life. During the time that I was incapacitated due to disease, this miracle began to manifest right in front of me. Living the Miracle means so much more than just defeating cancer. Living the Miracle now included getting rid of the idolatry of self-worth and doing everything I could for God's glory. Living the Miracle meant trusting my pastor to speak the truth into my life, even after I have lived for God all of these years. All of that is Living the Miracle. So what is God going to do on the other side of this trial? I am not sure, but I am sure I want to keep Living the Miracle the whole way through.

I said this before, but let me reiterate, my question throughout this process, is not "God, why do I have cancer?" That question is irrelevant. Why I have cancer I may never know. Nobody seems to have that answer. But the relevant question is this: "God, how do you want me to live through this process so that You will be glorified?" Do I feel good all of the time? No! But I don't have to complain about it either. Am I as productive as I want to be? No! But I can still do my part. My value isn't measured by how much I am able to get done. But I can be an encouragement to others just being me, Man from God.

CHAPTER 8

THE MIRACLE OF THE
CIRCLE OF PRAYER

My dear friend, Ernest Mitchell, during his personal devotion time, was reading about the children of Israel marching around Jericho. That particular day, he also happened to think of me, and he began to feel as though God might be leading him to do a "prayer circle." When he called Susan about it, he said, "I don't want you to think I am weird, but I think God has spoken to me about this." He asked her if it would be all right for him and some of our other friends to come to our house to pray. Like in the story of Jericho from his Bible reading, he felt that if they circled my house, the walls of cancer would come down! Of course, Susan said "Yes," and they collaborated to put together a day of prayer at our house.

Little did they realize how big this day would be. Little did I know at all, for they had kept it from me until that morning when Susan revealed simply that Earnest and a few friends were going to come pray for me. Earnest had invited a group of firefighters, sheriff deputies, police officers, and EMTs, who came out *en masse*. Susan and Earnest both had notified my children, grandchildren, sisters, my dad, and many other friends, right down to one of my bankers. The Brother's Keepers, an international firefighter's motorcycle group I ride with, were there in full regalia. In all, approximately 125 people circled our house that day.

As the people all prepared to pray, the Life Air helicopter broke into the sky, circling my house until it hovered up the driveway and brought me to tears with a salute, a helicopter front-dip maneuver after which they burst away. I was completely surprised and awed by everything that was happening. This particular sign of respect and honor is often performed at funerals; I don't know how often a Life Air crew does this for people who are alive. I still get emotional thinking or talking about this. I was so honored.

The helicopter's departure was the signal for the prayers to begin around the circle. One by one, each in turn around the circle, they began to pray. For approximately two hours, this wonderful group of friends prayed and prayed and prayed. All I could do was walk around, stand in front of each one, and listen to them pray. As I made my way around this circle, I noticed and remembered every single person, almost every single story uniquely connected to me in one way or another. I had been involved with them as a chaplain, had worked incidents with them, had preached weddings or funerals for them or their families, had supported their families at births or had managed a crisis with them in some manner. I had been with many of them to celebrate promotions and with others through times of defeat.

This experience was more powerful than can be expressed in words. Someone there took lots of pictures and Susan was able to make a magnificent book out of them. I look at it occasionally to remind me of the miracles of each person there and the miracles that are still taking place because of their prayers. The photobook is a beautiful, detailed account of what happened that incredible day, but to understand the power of the moment, you had to have been there.

There was one man in the back yard section of the circle, whose reaction I will never forget as long as I live. Without any prompting, he had fallen to his knees on our back patio, crying out to God over and over, "Father, forgive me." The power of God's presence was just that strong. And I mean this with all my heart: if that man got his life right with God, then having cancer is worth it for me. If he went home and is now a God-man, his family is enriched. When he makes Heaven, it will make all of this worthwhile.

When you develop a sense of community in your life, from that point on, there are some people who are always there. I have been a responder all my life. Because I was so entrenched in being the responder, I have never been the recipient of so much grace, love, tenderness, and effort. This Miracle of the Circle of Prayer put me on the receiving end of great blessing, and for these twenty four months, I have learned a lot about how to be a recipient. Watching my friends gather and pray taught me things I could never have known without this season in my life. I am grateful to be, Living the Miracle, in such a circle of prayer, love, and care.

CHAPTER 9

THE MIRACLE OF COLITIS DIFFICIL (C. DIFF)

You might not have ever heard of the disease in this chapter, but neither had I, until a 28-day battle made sure I would never forget the name of *Clostridium Difficile Colitis* (C. diff), a ruthless, unmerciful killer.

By now, you are well aware that the cancer treatment itself was changing everything about our "normal" lives. However, when C. diff entered the picture, the doctors' prognoses suddenly turned from "He might have two years to live" to "He might not make it through the night." Even worse for the moment, Susan had to hear all this while I was completely unaware, for I spent the first five days of this traumatic event in and out of consciousness, tempting death by the minute. To understand a little better, imagine me intubated and unconscious: this picture explains why many elements from the following story have been reconstructed from the viewpoints of others. Durell Tuberville was all but gone.

Susan and I knew something was terribly wrong when my relentless diarrhea had me fainting on the toilet. Diarrhea was one of the side effects of the chemotherapy, so we had been managing it for quite a while. I would get dressed, go to the toilet, get dressed, and go to the toilet again, making messes all along the way. It was bad, but we were trying to get used to it. As a grown person, however, you don't think you will have to be taken care of like an infant. I just never imagined the possibility of my bodily functions being so out of control. During this particular episode, a day and a half or more of two-to-four-hour diarrhea stints were really taking a toll on me, so we finally called the oncologist to report it as potentially abnormal. Dr. Bob recommended Lomitil, which eased the symptoms but never seemed to stop them completely. Then, after a short time of partial relief, the condition got worse and went on for another week. Susan had been caring for me all by herself, so with the growing threat of my incapacitation (all 240 pounds of me), Susan began to realize a full blown fainting spell would put her in a lurch. Another call to Dr. Bob confirmed that we had better get help. If we could make it through one more night, he suggested an early morning visit to his office was in order. Otherwise, the ER would be necessary. Up all night, my body was like a sieve. Every ounce of anything that went in traveled straight through me uninterrupted. Painfully dehydrated and malnourished, making it to morning was a miracle in itself.

The worst happened as the sun came up and we tried to get ready for Dr. Bob's office. Giving my precious Susan a real scare, with eyes rolling back in my head, I finally collapsed. May 3, 2013 would now mark the most vicious round in this fight for my life. Susan immediately called Ernest Mitchell, our faithful friend who happens to live nearby and also happens to be the fire chief at Caddo Fire District 3. Without hesitation, he headed our way.

Somehow, in between my fade-in/fade-out moments, Susan managed to get me laid out across our bed and even called 911. How she did, I just don't know. All I know is that she is amazing. The 911 dispatcher radioed Fire District 3, whose chief, Ernest, was almost already to our house when he overheard the call. Shortly after Ernest arrived, the paramedics made it and transported us to Schumpert Highland Hospital, where I went straight to the Intensive Care Unit, where I lay unaware for days to come, my memory completely blacked out. Susan and the medical team were my miracle instruments for the next portion of the story. They were magnificent in attending to my every need.

Surprisingly, this death-bout had nothing to do with cancer. Flashing back to a few weeks earlier, two unrelated health episodes had occurred. First, I had an abscessed tooth, which an oral surgeon was kind enough to pull for me. Of course, as standard procedure in pulling the tooth and cleaning out the abscess, the surgeon prescribed antibiotics to kill the dangerous infection and prevent it from spreading. Then a week or two after that, as I was recovering from the abscessed tooth, I came down with a rectal abscess. For this, I had to see the rectal surgeon, who admitted me to the hospital for a surgical cleanout. Standard procedure in this process, too, calls for high powered antibiotics. The point here is simple but deadly. Too many doses of antibiotic in a short span of time can kill the good bacteria in a person's colon, leaving the body defenseless. Hence, the onset of *Clostridium Difficile Colitis*, or C. diff.

Back to the ICU, before we knew exactly what we were dealing with, the medical team started intravenous fluids, nutrients, and another antibiotic (this one—praise God—was designed to build up healthy bacteria in the colon). Basically, however, we were only in a wait-and-see phase. As my family waited, they suffered and saw me suffer terribly. Then after three or four separate colonoscopies, the doctors finally concurred that I had C. diff and began to formulate a plan. When I eventually regained consciousness, I saw so many medical staff and so many different surgeons and doctors that I had a hard time telling who was playing quarterback. Thankfully, I knew several of them personally. We had a great team, including a particular nurse anesthetist, Bill Bond, whom I would like to recognize for the blessing he was when I heard him praying for me while he was putting me under for the final colonoscopy, which lead to the diagnosis of C. diff. Each time they had done a colonoscopy, they had a particular colon disease in mind, which they felt sure they would find. This time was no different except that they made a discovery they weren't expecting.

Now that I am awake, the pain returns to the story, while the horrendous diarrhea, I am sorry to say, never left, though it was thickening up a bit. It was ugly and uncontrollable enough still that I wonder whether you really want to read about it here. Moreover and ironically, at this point, even with the diarrhea, my body was retaining fluid. I swelled up like a balloon until it seemed my skin could burst at any moment. The fluid had seeped outside the cell walls, in between the cells, due to a condition called third-staging. To be sure, I went into the hospital weighing 242 pounds, but during the highest point of retention, I weighed in at 282. My son Dustin had helped me onto the scales, and we could not believe what we were seeing. My lower extremities were swollen beyond what I could have imagined, and I began to get my first taste of Neuropathy, the painful tingling which afflicts my feet even today. At the same time, as I mentioned before and will mention again as the story develops, I had excruciating abdominal pain, unrelenting even after I made it out of ICU, where I stayed isolated about a week. Because of the dangerously contagious status of my C. diff, only Susan, our boys, and a few dear friends were allowed into the ICU, each of them in-turn sitting with me wearing masks, protective gloves, and gowns.

The pain had to be dealt with, and thankfully it was, but before I share that relief, you might like to hear how the swelling subsided. The treatment for this sort of fluid retention is diuretics, which after a few days of adjustments began to work. For this reason, I was grateful they had put a urine catheter in when I arrived at the hospital. About the same time we started the diuretics, however, the hospitalist insisted I had worn the catheter too long already, so they had it removed. They gave me a handheld urinal, but with bloating and discomfort, along with being weaker than ever before, I was embarrassingly unable to maneuver that thing correctly. That night I wet the bed, wet my clothes, and just peed all over everything. It was very disconcerting and humbling to lie in my own urine waiting for help to arrive, but the next morning, when the new shift nurse made it to my room, I begged her, "Would you please reinstall the catheter?" After she installed the new catheter, she came back in just a few minutes to find 1600cc in the bag. She emptied it and returned in a few more minutes to find the bag filled again. This happened several times until she seemed amazed at the amount of fluid I was releasing. It was no wonder I had been swimming in urine all night. The diuretics were working. As the swelling began to recede, I had never been so grateful for a catheter and diuretics in all my life.

Now back to the pain. I mentioned that the abdominal pain had to be dealt with, and it had indeed been dealt with. While I was beginning to retain fluid and swell so much, Dr. Bob suggested morphine for my pain, but Susan remembered I do not respond well to morphine. Therefore, they resolved to use Dilaudid, a semi-synthetic morphine. This would be administered through my porta-cath (which was already in my chest for the sake of the Chemo treatments, on hold for the moment). Remember, I was still in and out of mental awareness, so all these decisions had to be made for me. Using my porta catheter instead of the IV would insure that the Dilaudid began its work quickly. I remember clearly my nurse Shannon coming in to administer the dosage (Shannon happens to be a nurse whose family lives across the road from us). Shannon roused me to make sure I was aware. She also wanted me to know that even thought it would act quickly, the relief would only last three or four hours. I remember all this clearly.

It seemed to be only 30 seconds to a minute before the next experience. Even though most of my memory from my hospital stay is fuzzy at best, this I remember in vivid detail. I will remember it the rest of my life. I truly believe it was from God.

My bed lifted up and floated out a window. I remained in my bed and looked all around. In pitch dark, the bed and I were suspended in air. Beautiful black darkness surrounded me with brilliant stars and a cloudless, like a Montana night. It seemed as if I could see forever out into the universe. "Am I dying?" I asked the Lord and then continued to talk to Him, "If I am dying, I'm perfectly ok with that. I want to be with you. . . . But if I am not dying, I will live for you 150% better than I ever have." Then I lay quiet. At that point, I looked over the left side of my bed to behold a bright city. It was so bright I could not look at it very long. I saw a street running right through the middle with buildings on each side. The brightness of it made me roll back in my bed. But then I looked again, and it was still there. Again, I asked God, "Am I dying? . . . If I am, I am ok with that. But if I am not, I will live for you 150% better than I have." This time I added, "However, I am not choosing! I am not asking you for more time, and I am not asking you to be in heaven, you decide."

At that point, the bed floated back in to the room and landed where it belonged. I could hear Susan saying to Shannon, "I can't understand what he's saying. He's never done this before." I was at total peace.

Then I drifted off to sleep, and I have been at total peace with my situation ever since. Why am I here today? Because the Lord has a plan for all of our lives even if we do not know or search for it. Being subject to that journey is what we are about. I am here today to tell you that God is real! I believe Heaven is real, and I believe I saw it.

The issue at hand today for those of us who have a cancer diagnosis is how are we going to live for God in such a way, that people are encouraged and motivated and blessed, and be able to say, "Look what God has done!" It is nothing that I have done.

There are many who have this diagnosis and are on the same regimen that I am on, but I want to live out the plan that He has for me. I understand more of what the Apostle Paul meant when he said, "to live is Christ and to die is gain." There are times when it would have been much easier for me to have died. Some of the pain and struggle would have been spared me, however, having gone through that and having had that experience, I am more at peace than I have ever been. So from that point on, I stayed in the hospital about three more weeks.

I was beginning to have a few good days, so Susan felt comfortable going across the street to a hotel to spend the night (The hotel room is another miracle . . . for another chapter). The first night, everything that could happen in the unit must have been happening because no one was available to respond to my call for help. My bowels decided to move two or three times within a short time, and I couldn't do anything about it. I just had to lie there in it until finally, after several hours, I decided, "I am getting up out of this bed to take a shower and get cleaned up." I had not stood on my own all this time, but somehow I managed to get myself upright, with the IV pole and catheter bag in hand. I was standing at the end of the bed when Susan walked in: "What are you doing!!" I showed her my bed, "I have been laying in this mess and I am going to take a shower."

I took a shower. Susan took care of the bed and the staff were finally able to stop and help. Looking back, I am so sorry I scared Susan like that. I wish I had thought it through better. But we made it and we learned that it was time for me to start moving around a bit. One of the doctors also suggested it was time for me to try to walk, so Susan contacted a dear friend who worked as a physical therapist at the same hospital. Stan secured a walker for me, and my recovery began.

"What's the worst that could happen?" I asked myself at the daunting thought of walking. "Well," I answered myself, "You could fall down and they would have to come pick you up." So I started. My first adventure was to the door and back. Several times a day, Susan and I made this trek, which was as far as I could go. I was weak, still swelled up a little, and neuropathy had settled in on my feet. It was painful and I had a tingling sensation all the time. Josh and Dustin were alternating staying with me during the day, so they and Susan would walk with me as far as I was comfortable going. I gradually built up stamina to walk out the door, turn left and walk 25 or 30 feet down the hall. When I made it back from these extreme journeys, I would get right in to bed until I recovered and got up to do it again. I would try to do that twice a day, mostly having to force myself to get up and do it. The farther I walked, the better I seemed to get.

My system seemed to be responding to the exercise. Eventually, my IV was removed and I was able to start a liquid diet. Then I graduated to solid food and was overjoyed to realize it was staying down and in! Praise the Lord. C. diff was going away. That was miraculous. My need for a hospital setting came to a close, but I still needed rehab, so that research began.

I only needed about a week at a rehab facility, and our good friend, Bubba Manning, owns a nice one right in the middle of a beautiful pecan orchard. This would prove to be an intensely rewarding week, as the physical and occupational therapists took me from walking the few steps I could muster on my own with a walker to being able to walk outside for the first time in a month. I was so excited to be outside with the sun on my face, and looking back, I could never express my gratitude to the therapist who let me walk outside even though she had her concerns about the uneven terrain. She was so excited when we came back indoors, she announced to everyone, "Durell walked outside!" Within a few days, I was lapping the facility, an extra lap every day until it was time to check out and head home. I was so glad to be able to push myself and get my body back on track; after all, I was supposed to be fighting cancer.

What a glorious day it was when Susan was able to take me home! She and I stood in the house and hugged and cried just to be together and back in our house. I still looked like death on a cracker, my face was sunken in, and I had dropped to 213 pounds, but I was as happy as could be to be home. C. diff had done its worst, and God had gotten us through.

I tell all this because it is truly miraculous. First of all, the level of C. diff I had is a killer, and those who survive it do not generally regain their strength this soon. The occupational therapist who followed up with me at the house (helping me learn to tie my shoes and giving me a neat tool to help button my own shirt) told us she had had C. diff before, and it took a year for her to recover. I was just a month into this and walking laps around our property. The C. diff did try to return twice, but we were able to identify it quickly and with the proper antibiotics and by eating probiotic rich foods like yogurt (I've never been a fan of yogurt until now), we were able to stop it before it got out of hand. Each time was an inconvenience and slowed my cancer-fighting progress down, but the threat to my life was over.

During the worst part of this whole ordeal, when I was still unconscious and doctors could not promise a happy ending, Susan recalls a conversation that truly defines our lives. My close friend David Glass came by the hospital to check on me and see if there was anything he could do. Standing at the end of my bed, in a difficult moment of reality, Susan asked him, "David, do you think he is going to die?" David answered, "We are just going to continue to pray!" I cannot tell you how many prayers were prayed for me during these 28 days, but I know that prayer made all the difference.

As soon as I had a chance to go to church, even though I had to wear an immunity protecting mask and sit in an isolated "crow's nest" seat with just me and Susan, I wanted to be there to show the Lord how grateful I was. I was grateful for every medical professional, for every friend, for every prayer, for every minute of this fight, which was now declared over, with the Lord as the victor. He had chosen for me, allowing me to live, and as I had promised, if I got to Live the Miracle, I was going to do it 150% better than I had ever lived before!

CHAPTER 10

COLITIS DIFFICIL (C DIFF)

by Susan Tuberville

After yet another trip to Houston, Durell developed an abscessed tooth. It ended up he had been prescribed pain meds for his radiation but was having to take them for the pain this tooth was causing. As soon as we returned, he was scheduled for an extraction—oral surgery. They put him to sleep, took out the offending tooth, and sent him home with a major antibiotic.

Shortly after he won the battle with the abscessed tooth, he began to experience an even greater pain in the rectal area. Bowel movements were excruciating; he would leave the bathroom white as a sheet and clammy to the touch. Many times he looked to be on the verge of passing out. What we found out was the radiation had caused a rectal ulcer which had become infected—you guessed it, another high dose of a major antibiotic. The symptoms, however, did not dissipate and the same surgeon, we had visited initially, examined him once again.

He would have to go in and clean the area out. We went in for a day-surgery to take care of the infected lesion. The following days and weeks run together from here for me. Durell continued to have major pain; they talked at one point about using hyperbaric oxygen chamber therapy for healing as the abscess in the rectum remained unhealed and excruciatingly painful.

Diarrhea had become a problem, which we attributed to the radiation and chemo combination. Durell was having difficulty even getting to the toilet in time. On top of these issues, his prostate trouble had returned with a vengeance. Medications were changed and increased, new meds added. His bowel movements were plagued by spasms, and he had bladder spasms on top of that. The list of meds was growing weekly while we continued to add new symptoms and problems.

After we consulted the oncologist about his level of pain and difficulty in voiding, he sent us to the urologist. The urologist treated Durell for bladder spasms and a bladder infection. He drained the bladder with a catheter, which Durell wore home. Also, in order to "get a jump on" the infection, the urologist gave him an injection of Rocephin and a prescription for another major antibiotic. By that evening, the diarrhea had turned into something else completely. Now we were dealing with what is termed chronic incontinence. Again, as far as we could tell, we were experiencing side effects of his chemo/radiation regimen, and by now we had added violent vomiting. From April 30th when we came home with the catheter, until May the 3rd, we worked around the clock just trying to manage the diarrhea, pain, and vomiting. Dr. Bob had told us if we could make it until Monday morning, to come straight to the cancer treatment center where he would give Durell an IV for loss of fluids and dehydration. Otherwise, I was to take him directly to the emergency room.

By 6:00 a.m. that Monday morning, I was on the phone with a friend who happens to live nearby and is also a fire chief and paramedic. I asked if he would assist me in getting Durell to the car, to which he offered to come right that moment. However, since the Cancer Treatment Center did not open until 8a.m. and Durell wanted to get himself somewhat presentable, I asked him to wait and come around 7a.m. By the time I hung up and got back to the bathroom, Durell was passing out on the toilet. We eventually got him to the bed, and I called 911, realizing now we could not transport him in my vehicle.

Praise God for Durell, for his strength, for our family, for his friends. Yes, Durell's never-say-quit attitude, our sons and daughters-in-law, and his (our) friends, as well as our oncologist were the ones who got me through the next month. Our oldest son, Josh, was headed home from Arkansas to see about his dad for himself, and when I called our youngest, Dustin, he met me at the hospital. Durell was transferred to the ER by the local fire department, who were also personal friends. What a reassurance it was to me for friends to be the ones to transport and work on Durell.

At the ER, the medical team determined he was in atrial fibrillation, his heart rate 220 and even higher at times. The diarrhea was still a constant problem, but they were more concerned with his heart. After talking to our boys, I called our pastor, and even greater waves of prayer and support began to pour in.

Durell was transferred to the Critical Care Unit where he was under the care of a hospitalist, a cardiologist, a gastrointestinal specialist, and his oncologist. Our journey had just gotten rockier.

The diagnosis of colitis difficile (C. diff) was made quickly, and as a result, Durell was quarantined. Anyone coming into the room had to glove and gown and dispose of the same upon leaving. For the first three weeks, visitors were restricted to immediate family. The hospital was wonderful about overlooking visiting hours (only 30 minutes every four hours) while I stayed with Durell around the clock, usually with one or both of our sons. However, the support of visitors coming to the waiting area continued to pour in. People prayed together in the waiting room, prayed with Josh and Dustin and myself, and prayed for Durell without ceasing. I was glad when we finally got a sign-in book so I would know who came when I was unavailable.

Watching the love of my life be reduced to dependence on those around him may have been harder for me than it was for him. This man exudes strength. This man **is** confidence. This man has a charisma and persona that demand respect! Durell just has to walk in to a room to fill it up. He embodies the exuberance and love of Christ in every cell of his being. He projects all the characteristics of a man who has the world by the tail. But for the next several weeks, he was as weak as a newborn. He had to have assistance with every detail of life. There were times I wanted to play one of his speaking-engagement DVDs for these caregivers so they would know who they were taking care of. Durell speaks motivationally in front of hundreds at a time, he personally directs disaster scenes on a national level, and he holds congregations spellbound when communicating the Gospel. "This man you see is not the man he is!" my spirit wanted to shout! But, it didn't matter. God spoke through Durell's spirit to everyone around him. And although they had no idea "who this man was," without exception, they treated him with great respect during a very humbling period in his life. By the time Durell was released from the hospital to rehab, he had forged the same respectful relationships with these doctors, nurses and aides that he inspires everywhere he goes. They all loved him.

Twenty-eight days in the hospital left Durell in a diminished physical condition. He was evaluated for home health services, had a walker and a bedside commode, and came home with Depends Undergarments and seventeen prescriptions to take throughout each day. We moved him to a bedroom we thought would offer the best accommodations for his current needs, and I set my phone alarm to his medicine schedule, which went every 3-4 hours around the clock. We began trying to get our lives back. C. diff is a cruel, hard disease, and everyone continued to tell us that this trial was not cancer related. However, had the radiation not caused the lesion, had the chemo not compromised his immunity, he never would have contracted it. This particular challenge was due to strong antibiotics on three different, unrelated occasions, destroying the good bacteria in his colon so the bad bacteria took over. And take over it did!

The physical demands on me as the caregiver were high. The mental demands to keep up with all the information, symptoms, treatments, and recommendations were higher and that was just the health pressures. Of course, the normal issues of life were present, as well; only now instead of two of us to address them, there was only me . . . though I was not alone! God's presence was very real to us both, and family and friends were ever available! Were it not for family, friends, and God's faithfulness, we would have had a much more difficult time.

C. diff is a nightmare. Its reoccurrence is not only common but expected when someone has it as bad as Durell had. We lived with the ever present reality of being on high alert. Our sons, Josh and Dustin, came to the house and bleached every surface before we returned home. I am so proud of our sons, but I think I have never been more proud than when I saw everything they had done. When I began to express that to them, they were so humble. They just said, "Well mom, we knew when you did get home you would not rest until it was done. And we know you need to rest, too." I became a 'germ-o-phobe' of the highest order.

I was also obsessed with Durell's nutrition. What could he eat? What could he keep down? At one point in the hospital, his liver went into failure from a lack of nutrition, and he was starving. They put him on liquid nutrition through an I.V. for a period of time, and he lost significant amounts of weight. I watched his face shrink, his eyes sink deeper into their sockets, and his lips draw away from his teeth. I remembered all too well watching this same transformation in his dear sweet mother as she moved into the final stages of dying. I asked the doctors if he was dying, and they believed for a while that that was a definite possibility.

Bringing him home alone scared me, I was afraid I could not do enough to keep him safe from relapse. I realized once again the value of friends, the value of people who were like-minded in faith and believed in prayer. God was so good to us. He wrapped his loving arms around us again and again through the physical arms of men and women who loved us.

This was not the end of the physical challenges, but it was by far the most critical and most difficult. Once we made it through the month of May, with only two mild recurrences of C. diff, we felt as though we could make it through anything.

CHAPTER 11

THE MIRACLE OF A SUPPORTIVE SPOUSE

You have heard of guys who "outkick their coverage." I'm one of those guys. At twelve years old—the summer before 8th grade—I met a girl who was and still is out of my league. We were at a church event, playing a game like musical chairs, during which each person had to kiss the forehead of the person in front of them. . . . That was all it took. The next school year, as just an eighth grader, I asked Susan to go steady with me, and we have been steady ever since.

As a sophomore in high school, I told my mom that Susan was the one for me. Of course, Mom thought I was too young to make such a big decision, but as far as I was concerned, the decision had already been made. Six years later (with all four of our parents on board by this time) Susan and I finalized our allegedly youthful commitment with solemn marriage vows. We were only 18 at the time, but here we are in our 50s, as committed as we ever have been. From those early days onward, Susan has been the one thing that completes me.

Back in 1977, a nice little two-bedroom, one-bath, 900 square foot house was only about $20,000, a brand new 2-door car cost $5,500, and gas was a whopping 36 cents a gallon. Times have certainly changed, but Susan has been as constant as anyone you could ever know. She has always been wonderful. She is consistent, organized, meticulous, purposeful, tender, compassionate, loving, giving, and slow to speak . . . . The list of her attributes goes on and on. I, on the other hand, have always been a cantankerous cuss. When they said "opposites attract," you can bet they were talking about me and Susan. She has loved and served God selflessly her whole life, while I pretty much lived for whatever pleased Durell.

If you want to know even more about what kind of woman Susan is, she graduated top of her class at Louisiana State University—Shreveport, where she attended on an academic scholarship. She has immaculate recall and, frankly, could have been anything she wanted to be. From the time she was just a girl, what she wanted to be was a pediatrician. However, after marrying me, she decided that a pediatrician's schedule might keep her from being home with her own children the way she desired, so she changed her plans and went into Education, a field where she could still help kids but also be home for her own kids. That was a sacrificial choice which she did not have to make. Instead of pursuing her first dream, she created another, eventually becoming a counselor for the public school system where she would spend every day helping children and their families. Twice she was named Caddo Parish Counselor of the Year, once for Elementary and later for Middle School. That's the kind of lady Susan is.

If it were not for Susan, I would still be an unruly old trouble-maker. In 1978, we were at a crossroads in our marriage. The way things were going, Susan could have kicked me out of the house, and no one would have blamed her. But she didn't. She displayed great patience as she, along with my mom, prayed for me every day. One day, however, she finally had to tell this rabble-rousing husband of hers to make a decision: either we were going to be "us," or Durell was going to keep up his "huntin', fishin', and fightin'" out there on his own. The choice was mine. I easily realized at the time that without Susan, my very life could be in jeopardy (I'm leaving lots of details out of the story, but suffice it to say, I used to get myself into real trouble). Furthermore, I also realized that I didn't just need her, I wanted her, and I wanted a family with her.

Then in March of 1979, Susan announced we were having a baby. That night I could not sleep. I went to the bathroom and stared at the man in the mirror: "What characteristics do I have that I would want a son to have?" Only one good quality came to mind: I was a hard worker. Then I walked out onto our porch at 2622 Lakehurst Avenue and stared up at the night sky. Looking at the bright stars, I prayed the best way I knew how: "If You are the God my wife and momma keep trying to convince me You are . . . if You will forgive me, I will live for You the rest of my life." The Bible says a "believing wife" should always pray for and keep being an example to her wayward husband, in hopes that he will eventually come around. That night, alone on my front porch, while my wife and brand new yet-to-be-born baby slept quietly in our little house, I saw those scriptures come to pass. Her patience and example had brought me to Christ.

When I finally got everything right between me and God, Susan and I had a new confidence that we would never part from each other. From now on, if she ever did get tired of me, I would simply tell her: "If things get so bad you need to leave . . . just remember, I'm coming with you." That was the mantra of my new commitment to our relationship. Now we would be together come what may.

Then cancer came. The first time we were struck with cancer, Susan was the target. She had been having abdominal pain which led doctors to perform a normal, non-invasive gall bladder test. If this test had revealed the root of the problem, they would have just taken her gall bladder out laparoscopically. However, since the test failed, they kept looking and eventually found a cyst on her pancreas. This was our first experience with a medical miracle. While the surgeons had her opened up to perform a Whipple procedure, they found that her gall bladder was indeed diseased, but also they discovered that the growth on her pancreas was a precancerous cyst which bisected her pancreas.

You might wonder, "What was the miracle in that?" Well, to put it in a nutshell, if the first round of tests had been a success, they would have removed the gall bladder . . . and Susan would have died within 18 months. You see, pancreatic cancer sadly is not normally discovered soon enough to save a person's life. This was a miraculous diagnosis because it did save her life. Frankly, it didn't just save her life; it saved mine, too, because God knew I would never beat my own future cancer without Susan by my side. Eleven years after Susan's victory over what could have become pancreatic cancer, I found out about my cancer. Thank God, Susan is still here to be my rock, my greatest support, my prayer warrior, my comforter, encourager, listener, and absolute best friend.

Every time we go to a doctor visit, Susan carries a notebook with the chronology of our whole journey. She has been my "detail" person the whole way through. When we visit a medical professional, I don't ask a lot of questions: intense quizzing of physicians is just not my way. But Susan asks everything. As a person of great intellect, she will keep asking questions until the answers make sense to her. Left up to me, our position would have been, "Whatever it is, it is, and that's what it's going to be. We will just deal with it." Susan, on the other hand, wants to know everything the doctors know, and more. Remember, one of her first questions after we received my diagnosis was whether or not this disease was hereditary. She had immediately realized that we needed to know this for the bigger picture (whether or not our sons had anything to worry about). This is the sort of issue Susan is always sure to get to the bottom of. Honestly, that part of who she is saved me. I would not be where I am now without her meticulous personality.

Sometimes, married couples see personality differences—like this one between me and Susan—as a blight on their relationship. Well, I say thank God for personality conflicts.

Sometimes, they can save your life! When people get into situations like this whole cancer treatment process, it is very easy to "major on the minors" or to look at our spouse through overly critical lenses. If he/she does, or does not do, something to our liking, we snap at them or clam up. All of us are guilty of this at times, but one thing we need to realize is that there is good reason for our spouse to be different from us. They might not ever do anything the same way we would do it. At first glance, this can hinder a relationship, but you just never know how important it might be that the two of you do not think alike.

When Susan and I had to talk about the idea of only having two more years on this earth together, you better believe each of us had our own way of seeing the situation. However, making a big deal out of our differences would have made the tough situation even tougher. Whether we saw things the same or not, we had to fight this fight together, not fight each other. In this battle, we had a common enemy, which was enough to make our own differences much less important. That made all the difference.

Having a two-year life expectancy, by the way, can crush a person's emotions. An onlooker's first thoughts might naturally focus on the emotional struggle of the person with the cancer, but in reality, the strain of this diagnosis can destroy the spouse, too. I thank God that on several different occasions, Susan and I were able to talk in depth about how we wanted to deal with this prognosis emotionally. I wanted to know what was important to her during this process, and she felt the same way about me. We had to come to an understanding on some key issues. For instance, how would we pray? Or what would we say to others? It might be terrible to have only two years left, but how do we want to live these next two years? We sat together on the porch and cried. We sat together in the living room and cried. We held each other in the doctor's office, and cried. Then, together, we decided, "If we only have two years . . . or if we only have two months . . . or if we only have 20 minutes, let's just live! Let's be happy with what life we have left." That would be our emotional agreement.

When we had to come up with an aggressive game plan of faith and medicine to defeat this horrible circumstance, Susan offered me her aggressive agreement. She simply said, "Whatever you want to do with this, I am in. I am committed." So we agreed together on a high level of faith and an all-out medical fight, using as powerful a chemotherapy cocktail as the doctors had to offer. When people asked how we were doing, our answer would be "Living the Miracle." When people wanted to know what we were doing about the cancer, we would tell them about the great doctors and medicine which were on our side and the power of prayer which we trusted with all of our hearts. The power of agreeing together made all the difference.

The value of having the agreement of your spouse cannot be overstated. So often, cancer patients are attended to with such fervor that the spouse is almost overlooked. If they are overlooked, they become relegated to the position of spectator, when in reality they are probably the one working the hardest. What a tragic irony for the primary caregiver to be seen as a spectator! If I could stress just one thing to married couples going through this traumatic life event, it would be this. It is absolutely necessary to acknowledge the value of our spouses as they participate in this entire process. The patient is often unaware of how much his or her spouse goes through and how much would never work out right if the spouse had not been involved. Even when you are hurting your worst, it is good to look up and let your spouse know how much you appreciate that they are going through this with you.

If you are a cancer patient, take time to encourage your spouse. It will make you feel better yourself. It makes me feel better. It has helped me manage my cancer treatment process. Susan has not wavered through this process. Surely, there have been many more struggles in her heart and mind than I will ever know about because she is very good at resolving things her own way, within her own time. However, encouraging her in tangible ways whenever I can has still helped me manage myself. I am not the greatest homemaker, for instance, but when Susan has gone to work all day, while I am home with my infusion pump, I try to get supper ready or do some of the chores I can handle. Do I feel good physically? No. But when it is all said and done, she will walk through the door into a clean house, sometimes even with supper on the table, and she will know that I appreciate her. Honestly, anything I can do to lighten her load lightens mine. If something makes her feel better, it makes me feel better. Considering how weak I have been at times, unable even to walk to my own mailbox or get up to do much at all, helping with chores is not always possible, but to do what I can lets Susan know that I am with her as much as she has had to be here for me.

If you are a cancer patient, you will feel better getting the focus off yourself. What better way to do that than to start with your spouse. Focus on what you can do for him or her on your good days. I knew that the second weekend after each treatment, I was going to feel my best physically, so I tried to plan things with Susan on those dates. I could go to work when I was fatigued and hurting, but I wanted my time with Susan to be during my prime moments. In some psychological and emotional way, it helped me to manage my cancer treatment plan and Live the Miracle. Part of the miracle of healing is having that significant person there through thick and thin, so don't they deserve the best times as much as they have served during the worst?

In our case, Susan did not only have to take care of me during my utter physical impairments and the extra household duties, but she also stepped up to take care of my business affairs. There were times I was completely out of touch with everything, not even aware of my own existence. Susan had to meet with my office manager and tackle problems she had never faced before. She just had to find things (like our business checkbook, of all things) and figure them out. Until the C-diff episode, we had not imagined that I would be entirely incapacitated, but at that time, it became imperative that we not fall behind on bills and mortgage notes associated with keeping our business afloat. She handled things far better than I would have if I had been in her same predicament. My system of managing these things is unique to me, but she managed to pull everything together and make it work. To her credit, she and Craig, my office manager, kept our business stuff going without one whisper from me. She did a tremendous job. There are not enough words in my vocabulary to say Thank You for that.

No one likes the morbid turn which has to be taken in discussions like these, but another issue Susan had to face is what would happen if I died. Luckily, years ago we had started an End of Life book. This book lists all of our properties, our insurance policies, our bank account information, etc. It even details how we would like our funeral services to transpire, like which songs to play and who should preach the eulogy. We did not want to dwell on these issues, but I have brushed close enough to death to know that a book like this is invaluable. Our boys can read each of these books and know exactly what our living wishes were. We spent several hours reviewing this book together shortly after my diagnosis because we wanted it to be as up to date as possible. Of course, having this information helped Susan to be more at ease, and I do suggest that everyone work up some sort of End of Life book for your spouse and loved ones. One thing about the future is that it will always be unknown. Do whatever you can to take the uncertainty out of the unknown.

Finally, I would like to take a moment to talk about celebrating our spouse while we have a chance. As a matter of celebration, I want to say—out loud—all the things which ought to be said. The thought might be nice, but your spouse needs to hear your appreciation. I want to make deliberate statements of gratitude and acknowledgement. "Thank you for making pancakes this morning." "Thank you for cooking a nice lunch." "Thank you for washing my clothes." "Thank you for all the things you do because you care." If we focus on our own suffering, we will lose focus on our spouse and the gifts and miracles of our day-to-day life. Because I have experienced this personally, I know at times, the suffering of cancer and disease is unbearable. However, choosing to honor and value our spouse is more important than we could ever realize.

After recovering from C diff (the life-threatening bacterial disease unrelated to my cancer; see chapter 9) and gaining some of my strength back, I began to wonder what I could do to show my appreciation for Susan publicly. I wanted my friends and staff to know how grateful I am for her personal sacrifices. She is not one who likes public attention or adoration, but I had to violate that just this once. My friend Bobby who owns a wonderful local restaurant—Johnny's Catfish—provided a perfect room and splendid dinner in order to celebrate "The Miracle of a Supportive Spouse." Hundreds of invitees eagerly reserved their spots to express the same sentiments I was feeling, but most of all, I was the one who wanted to tell the story of her faithfulness. I am so proud to call Susan my wife, and I am proud to tell everyone about the Miracle of a Supportive Spouse.

CHAPTER 12

THE MIRACLE OF FRIENDSHIPS

If I could name them all, I would. Some remain nameless because I was not even conscious when they came to my aid. Others I just cannot name because this chapter would turn out to be too long with stories. Honestly, there is no way to include all the stories of all the friends who became miracles to me during this battle with cancer. Some of these friends have been life-long, while others I didn't even know personally, until they blessed me with the benevolence of their friendship. These countless numbers of friends stepped in during my time of need and proved to me that Friendship truly is a Miracle. These pages are dedicated to their kindness and compassion.

Friendship has always been important to me. I suppose this personality trait is part of what led me to become a chaplain, pastor, and counselor. Having served in one or more of these roles since age twenty-one, I have had lots of time and opportunities to develop lasting friendships.

As a funny fact, this hasn't always appeared to be a blessing to my family. My boys might even have called it a curse. You see, my sons grew up without being able to go anywhere in our town without running into someone who knew me. Imagine being a teenage boy, feeling like your dad has hundreds of spies all over the city keeping up with your every move. "We can't go anywhere that Daddy doesn't know somebody!" they would moan. It was quite funny from my perspective, but they would like to have had a little more freedom, I am sure. They grew up with a nice, healthy fear that whatever they did could easily get reported back to me. I loved every minute of it—not the torture my boys endured, but the chance to invest in and really get to know so many different people as friend and encourager.

I cannot tell you how many times over the years, Susan and I have been approached with familiar smiles, each time to find out that I had helped this person during a tragic moment or a difficult circumstance. Often, someone will say, "You probably don't remember me, but . . ." Then they will recount a tragedy which befell their family, reminding me of the role I played during their trauma and recovery. I have never taken a single one of those conversations for granted because they define what I have wanted my life to be about—sowing peace into the lives of others during their hours of grief and hardship.

A miraculous side-effect of this personality trait of mine is the topic of this chapter in my journey. Suddenly, now that Susan and I were facing the crisis of terminal cancer, people's love and friendship began to sprout up everywhere. The scriptures clearly teach about "sowing and reaping." Whatever sort of seeds a man plants in the ground is the sort of harvest he should expect to grow. Well, this miracle certainly came to pass in my life. Everywhere Susan and I went—restaurants, the movies, the grocery store, or wherever—people would stop us, but now, instead of recounting the time that I might have helped them, they were all offering hands of friendship to me. Honestly, there must have been thousands of people praying for me. I never went anywhere without hearing, "Aren't you Durell Tuberville? Hey, we have been praying for you! You're on our church prayer list!" I was seeing a harvest of friendship grow right before my eyes.

Not only were people offering prayers and concern for me, but acts of service and generosity also began to pepper every portion of our story. From showing up to groom our lawn or wash our car, to providing a meal or even raising thousands of dollars to help with medical bills, the friendships of my life suddenly became miraculous. Friends from the community, guys and gals from the Fire Department, members from church, and people from every facet of life began to minister to me and Susan. They genuinely came to our rescue. You just never know how nice it is for someone to bring you firewood until you are laid up and unable even to strike a match on your own. We will never forget the kindness of all these friends. From the gracious offer of our dear friends Mack and Teresa Praytor to let us use their home when we had to visit the hospital in Houston to the consistent company of David, Sandy, Leland, Timbo, Mark, and so many others who spent hours at the hospital with me, reminiscing, telling stories and jokes, and entertaining the nurses. Sometimes my friends would just sit and watch TV while I slept. Whatever the depth of commitment, suddenly, I had help from everywhere and would not have to spend even a moment of this trial alone.

Especially during my chemo treatments, these visits meant the world to me. Seldom did I go to the hospital on treatment days that friends didn't show up. The volunteer ladies at the hospital always came by to offer me the hospital lunch, but almost every time, I already had a buddy on his way to bring something for us to eat together. During these 8-hour treatments, we would laugh and carry on. The nurses on my wing of the facility finally concluded that they had never seen a chemo patient have so much fun getting treatments. We would be the loudest room in the hospital. These guys could shoot the bull with me forever. As a very sociable personality, I need people around me, so their willingness just to be present meant the world to me.

Of course, there came many times when their presence meant the difference between life and death. I already told the story of Ernest being the first responder when I became incapacitated by C-diff. Then there were guys like Tim Thames, Reggie McElhannon, and Carl McBeath who came to the hospital and provided Susan reprieve even though they were very aware of the highly contagious nature of this strain of bacteria, which almost killed me. Timbo, a wiry ball of energy, also happens to be an avid note-taker with a good bit of medical knowledge, so he was able to relieve Susan, who was in dire need of rest at this stage of the game. Tim stayed with me all night in the hospital making sure the hospital staff honored the doctor's orders for me not to be disturbed too often. I cannot express how much we appreciate the peace of mind and freedom these men provided for Susan.

Speaking of Susan's need for rest, another miracle of friendship occurred during this tumultuous time with the C-diff episode. We live about 20 to 30 minutes from the hospital, so for Susan to "run home real quick" was just not feasible, especially considering the state of constant emergency I was in. That is when a longtime friend of mine, Michael Perser, a captain on the Shreveport Fire Department, pulled together some other fellows to help. One of my staff members, fellow counselor Patti Bornaman, had pointed out the problem to him, and he ran with the solution. Michael, along with another fireman John Davis, spearheaded an effort to raise money for Susan to stay at the Hampton Inn, right across the street from the hospital! Several firefighters jumped on board, and before long, they collected enough money for Susan to stay eleven days. From that moment on, without having to leave the vicinity, Susan could break away a few minutes at a time, take a nap, shower, or just regroup her emotions. Also, our son Josh was also able to use the room when he came in from out of town.

What a miracle friendships were turning out to be!

Two of my buddies, Tim and Mark called me on one of my good days: "Gather your stuff up. We are going to Arkansas." So that's exactly what we did. On a non-treatment weekend, they took me on a road trip—including a three-mile foot-hike into the mountains—not knowing whether I could even last. I was quite a bit slower than they were used to, I'm sure, and I had to stop to catch my breath a lot, but I was so grateful that they would make something like this happen. It was just the kind of experience I needed to gain perspective (i.e., climbing a mountain when I knew I couldn't). Here I was having to pray for every step up this mountain, but I had my two friends to lean on (I leaned on a lot of trees that weekend, too). I learned lots of lessons that weekend, but mostly I grew even more to appreciate this miracle of friendship.

Another weekend, one of my other buddies, Rusty, called me: "We are going fishing." That weekend (a "good" weekend) several of us had a blast bass fishing on Lake Fork in Texas. Then there's all the pond fishing I got to do with my friend David Glass and the target shooting I had so much fun doing with my friend Buddy. I guess a chapter on friendship in the Deep South has to include fishing and shooting stories. But this was not all just country-boy fun. Friends like retirees John Fulco and Leland McNabb came up with all kinds of ideas of how they could babysit me awhile. And one of my most memorable friendship moments is when Mark Richardson picked me up in his convertible corvette for a long drive through the country. I will never forget the long line of traffic behind us two old men driving down that two-lane highway at 40mph just to have fun. We would laugh and cut up as all the impatient young folks waited for the dotted yellow line so they could roar past us and get on with their busy little lives. Stopping for some good old country bar-b-q made me realize once again that friendship is worth slowing down for. What a good time.

Friendship means everything to me. I hope that these few little stories might encourage someone. Maybe someone will realize how important it is to invest in others, to be there for them during their hour of need. You never know when the shoe will be on the other foot. The Bible calls that "Sowing and Reaping." My prayer is that everyone will have beautiful friendships in this life. You never know how much it means to someone for you to offer to cook them a meal or to mow their yard. In my line of work, I knew that I had developed lots of meaningful friendships, but I had never called on anyone for real needs of my own. I guess I had hoped I would never have to. But now that I was down, the friendships of my life grew up like a miracle harvest.

I would never wish cancer and chemotherapy on anyone, but rekindling of old friendships and building new ones might not have ever happened without my situation being what it is. I thank God for that miracle.

God continues to lay me and Susan on people's hearts, and we continue to count every friendship a miracle . . . every friendly contact a blessing straight from God. Here recently, we even struck up a friendship with a wonderful little massage therapist named Elaine. Come to find out, she had trained at M.D. Anderson, of all places, and acquired the specialty of giving massages to cancer patients. Talk about the miracle of friendship!

Friendships have made my cancer journey much more navigable. Susan and I do not know what we would have done without a community of people willing to meet some of our smallest needs, whether cooking a meal and running errands, or risking personal harm in order to stay with me in a quarantined hospital room. We thank God every day for the Miracle of Friendship.

CHAPTER 13

THE MIRACLE OF FAMILY

Having cancer or dealing with any serious illness, a person faces an untold number of uncontrollable, unplanned situations. From losing physical abilities to a lack of clarity in thought, life becomes unmanageable for the patient. Energy and desire both seem to desert you while fatigue begins calling the shots. That's when the "supporting cast" of the story begin to shine. I have already spoken about the miracle of friendship. No doubt, without my friends—old and new—this story would not read the same at all. Furthermore, I would never attempt a single line in this book without including a sole chapter devoted to Susan, my Miracle Spouse. However, if they hand out awards for best supporting cast of our story, my entire family will have to crowd the stage to make the acceptance speech. Hence, it is my highest honor to present to you The Miracle of Family.

I always knew my sons were gifts from God, but now through the most critical time of our lives, they have proven to be miraculous. Susan and I always tried to teach our boys that the world does not revolve around them. In other words, we wanted them to focus on the needs of others instead of whining about their own needs and desires. Of course, we never diminished them by any means; on the contrary, we taught them that they were vitally important to God's plan for this world, and we made sure they had opportunities to be involved in church and civic organizations which concentrate on taking care of others. Little did we know while training the boys this way that *I* would turn out to be the one in need. Now, with great humility, I call to mind the scripture, "Train up a child in the way he should go, and when he is old, he will not depart from it." I could not be prouder about anything else in my life: when I became incapable of taking care of myself, my boys proved they had not departed from the path. This time along that path, they found their dad . . . and they stopped to take care of me.

I thank God for Josh and Dustin. To put it simply, what they did when Dad became incapacitated was drop everything and just be there for Mom. As Mom found herself thrust into managing a world of unknowns, the boys took vacation days at work and time away from their businesses, stepping up to help mom face each issue as it came. They would sit for hours at the hospital so their mother could get some rest. Just to be able to leave that confined room for a few hours, to clear her mind in a hot bath or to do some nest-mending at home, she appreciated every minute. They encouraged her to do that and rotated their time to be most efficient.

The boys were there to help their mom make medical decisions. Treatment modalities and working with the physicians always presented difficult choices. Indeed, part of the constant dilemma looming ominously over Susan, especially during my battle with C-diff, was how to know the right way to go. When different medical professionals offer varying suggestions, a family can become confused, but our boys brought their minds to the task and talked things through until their mother would feel comfortable making a final call. When somebody presented a difficult decision to Susan, she and the boys would put their heads together and say, "What questions do we need to ask about this, and how do we want to proceed depending on each possible answer?" Susan would take copious notes from their brainstorming; then after it was all collaborated, the boys would support Susan, who was ultimately left with each choice. Without Josh and Dustin, Susan would have felt isolated at best, cut off from one of her personally better modes of decision-making, which is to bounce ideas around until she finds out which one bounces the best. Wow. What a miracle! The miracle of good and godly sons! This alone relieved much of the stress Susan faced while her husband lay bedridden and mostly unconscious.

It must be noted next, however, that our sons do not stand alone playing their role in this story. Please allow me to introduce you to my two miraculous girls, our precious daughters-in-law. Claleigh is married to Josh, and Lindsey is married to Dustin. These two supported their husbands while their husbands supported their mom while their mom supported their dad — or Pop as the girls call me. We never could have asked for more wonderful daughters. They had to take care of things on their own home fronts, with our grandbabies all young at the time, but they would call often to maintain a status report on us and to talk girl-talk with Susan so she could focus, however briefly, on something other than being my caregiver. These girls are gifts from God to our family.

Can you see why I call this the Miracle of Family? How could we have gotten through this trial without family?

Susan was also continually supported by her two sisters Dana and Jenny and my two sisters, Denise and Darla. These four girls always make phone calls or send text messages right at the right time. This support for Susan continues to be outstanding. Our extended family stands ready in the wings waiting to offer support whenever needed — often on the spur of the moment — to fill the gap with what we lack in order to get through the day. As everyone knows, families are not perfect, and I can tell you that my sisters and I have gotten crossways a few times in our lives, but when the chips are down, family is family. We are there for each other no matter what, right or wrong, thick or thin. Through our sisters and others, we have experienced this incredible miracle of extended family. When crisis times come, family will forget about themselves and focus on the one in need. One of my sisters' lives far away and the other one nearby. The one nearby cooks a lot, so she will often stop by to bring us something to eat (that's what we do in the South). My sister who lives far away calls or texts me often, reiterating her concern or support. Even just "I'm thinking about you today" can make a big difference to a brother who is facing the trial of his life. We are grateful for our sisters.

As mentioned in earlier chapters, I didn't have my mom to help me through this season. We lost her shortly after I was diagnosed. Mom had always been an anchor for me through difficult times, but I will never know how much her presence and touch would have helped me through this because she is not with us. As is the case with many young men and their dads, I have to admit—especially in my earlier years—my dad and I have been known to disagree and fuss with each other, but somehow none of those things matter when cancer enters the scene. From the drive to Houston in his plush handicap-fitted van, to those phone calls at just the right time, Dad has been a support in his way as well.

Fortunately, Susan's two sisters, Dana and Jenny, do the same in staying in touch. They communicate with each other or with me weekly and sometimes daily just to remind us of their support. This is truly a blessing to Susan as her parents passed away several years ago.

This support from extended family—especially in light of the relationship barriers which we sometimes face in our families—brings to mind another important scripture we have always held to as a family, and tried to teach our boys. The Bible says, "Don't let the sun go down on your wrath." In other words, don't allow yourselves to hold a grudge, to be upset, or to stay angry; don't allow yourself to go to bed discontent with your family. Love one another while you have a chance. We believe that practicing this philosophy as a family was imperative when we came to face this trial of cancer. In families, there will always be opportunities for offense, hurt feelings, anger, and even bitterness, but if these feelings are allowed to linger through the night, when a dark day dawns, the family's light can be snuffed out.

After what I have been through, I want to say to every family, whatever condition you find yourself in right now, start rectifying things that are wrong. Make apologies. Do whatever is necessary for the family to come together again. Utilize the gift of forgiveness. To forgive one another for mistakes, faults, and poor decisions, to focus on what we can do to become that family which supports and encourages one another, this is the Miracle of Family. We don't know when a crisis may occur. We don't know when one of us will be diagnosed with cancer. It certainly was not on my schedule to be diagnosed with Rectal Adenocarcinoma, Stage 4. It certainly was not in my life's plan to sit and listen to my physicians tell me the best they could hope for me was two years. At 55 years old, that was not a part of my family plan!

Had our family been in duress, we would not have been able to come together to make decisions and support one another. Our family is not perfect by any means, but we have stuck to a few principles which allowed this crisis to make us stronger rather than weaker. The miracle of family proved that fatigue and confusion can be overcome when a family has simply chosen to be a family. Families must choose to believe they are each other's greatest treasure, and to treat each other like it. Family is the greatest gift God has given us. This is something worth teaching our children, to treat family like fine china, like valuable crystal, like the most valuable treasure we can ever have. We must tend to it, strengthen it, coddle it, nurse it, and do all the things necessary to remind ourselves that the family is the miracle which will sustain us in the worst of times. Having gone through this experience, we can look back and say, because we came to each other's rescue, the Miracle of Family continues to grow. The experience of getting through a crisis revealed the paramount advantages of having a loving, caring, forgiving family. This crisis served our family, to make us stronger and better.

At the risk of overstating this principle, I want to say it even louder—the Miracle of Family cannot be overrated. The family is the most powerful relationship we will ever experience. The comfort and confidence of a supportive family makes the impossible possible. I hope reviewing my family's story helps us all to ask ourselves what we are doing to make our families prepared for the next crisis. Can we manage a crisis together? What are we doing today to be ready for the unknowns of tomorrow? Are we assuring our family of our loyalty and faithfulness, or are we letting our family drift apart because of disagreements and differing personalities? Do I need to swallow my ego and deny myself the right to hold a grudge? If I knew that my family member was going to be diagnosed with Stage 4 cancer tomorrow, how would I really want today's conversation to go? How much would I apologize for the words we exchanged yesterday?

Family should be the ones you can let your hair down around without fear of judgement. These are the people, after all, who will be changing out your bedpan and taking care of your basic needs. Somehow in the day-to-day, we ignore these realities. When a husband and wife first get together, they are so in love they think they could never live without each other. And when those precious little children come along, we parents cannot see ourselves doing anything else but taking care of them. However, as time goes on, we allow those relationships to be diluted with the busyness of life. When we rub each other the wrong way, instead of stopping the friction by holding each other tighter or dealing with the issue, we move away from each other. Then when crisis hits, we are ill prepared to address it.

What I want to recommend to every family is to make sure God is first, that His precepts are the guide of our homes. Getting along with each other is not about whether we want the same things, have the same goals, or have the same issues. Neither is it about whether we all respond the same to a given set of circumstances. It is not even about whether we all serve God with the same intensity or in the same manner. Rather, it is about allowing each individual to live in their own pursuit. As scripture makes clear, we should each pursue our own salvation, to prepare ourselves in our own desires to be like God the best we can. When we allow our families to separate because of differences, we succumb to an ironic tragedy because it should actually be our differences that make us useful to each other in a time of crisis.

Sometimes we allow ourselves to get in the habit of focusing on the things that are not the real issue or things that are not really important in the overall development of our relationships. It is all too easy to allow yourself to focus on the things that you perceive to be negative. To beg the question, do you think it would be fair for me to compare my sister who lives far away with the one who drops by the house often with a special dish she has prepared just for me? No. Those are just not comparable situations. But how often do we make these unfair judgments on family members? Family will judge each other on little things like this without rationally thinking through their feelings. Whether you feel neglected by the sister who is hundreds of miles away is not the issue. Your sister who lives a hundred miles away cannot realistically do more than send you an encouraging text. If you spend time stewing over little things, you lose sight of the bigger picture. Each family member needs to be free to show support in their own way and with the resources and abilities they each have at present.

The Miracle of Family is that we learn to appreciate and gravitate toward each person's support in whatever way they offer it. We celebrate each person's contribution to the solution rather than comparing them by saying one cares more and one cares less. The miracle of family happens when we stop focusing on inadequacies and, rather, begin to cheer for each other in whatever little things are done right.

These are all the precepts of God.

Truly, I have come to appreciate how short this life is, and I hope my experience can bring your family this revelation without the crisis. Make the commitment to be a better family member than you have ever been before. I want to look in the mirror each day I have left and accept the responsibility to be the best husband, the best father, the best father-in-law, the best grandfather, the best son, and the best brother I can be to my family. Therein lies the Miracle of Family—finding what I can do to make my family what it needs to be. I have one shot at building a family, period. Living through cancer has reminded me to live the Miracle of Family even more. I will not allow myself to focus on my struggles more than I focus on the needs of my family. One of the greatest parts of the success of Living the Miracle is focusing on things greater than and outside of my immediate cancer struggle. Family is the greatest of these focuses.

Closing this chapter, I want to point out that this supporting cast of family has not just sustained me when I could not sustain myself. It has also energized me to get up and continue sustaining others. Playing with the grandkids might wear me out more than it used to, but it also brings me life. To have our grandsons walk with Pop around the yard and to answer all their curiosities concerning my cancer treatment brings me the greatest joy. To get the chance to help one of my boys, or their families, fulfills me and makes me grateful every day. To do anything in the world for Susan after all she has done for me is all I need to make me want to wake up another day. This is the Miracle of Family.

Please let me encourage you if your family member is struggling with cancer, just be with them and surround them with family. Give them the reassurance that I was able to experience. Focus on each other's successes and give each other the benefit of the doubt. Moreover, if you yourself have been stricken with cancer, continue to reach out to your family. Let them know how much you need them.

Young families, before the crisis comes, remind your children of the vital role they play in your life and in God's kingdom. Teach them to focus on meeting needs greater than their own. Have a philosophy of care and compassion and trusting God for guidance in your relationships. Never allow a

"Don't bother me right now" season to touch your home. God is still in the miracle working business, and He wants your family to be miraculous.

In short, let the Miracle of Family work for you. It will sustain you when all else fails. And when the awards are handed out, your family will have to crowd the stage to make the acceptance speech.

CHAPTER 14

THE MIRACLE OF RECEIVING

According to the Myers Briggs Inventory of Personality, my Personality Type is "Inspirer," which means, among other things, I operate under a high desire to help others. The flipside of that coin is that I also find it difficult to receive help from others. With this personality type, to sit back while someone else does something for me is almost impossible. This explains the feeling of devastation I had when I drove into my driveway to find someone mowing my yard for me. Instead of feeling overjoyed, I was broken. For me, this act of kindness spoke directly to my lack of capability, my powerlessness, and my perceived reduction of manhood and ego. From that moment on, it would take a host of friends and family members to help me embrace the concept of receiving. Through a series of generous events, which I tried to avoid and tried even harder to preclude upon their suggestion, God began to open my eyes to see the Miracle of Receiving. It took a change of mind and spirit before the emotion of gratitude would overcome my feelings of helplessness.

The sudden inability to contribute effectively to any given situation is a side effect of cancer which no one seems to talk about. For me, however, this is one of the worst side effects. To know in your mind what needs to be done to keep the household running or to ward off financial disaster but to be completely sidelined physically will distress a patient's spirit. Speaking with other cancer patients, I have found this to be more prevalent than we might realize on the surface. The whole thinking process is challenged when we lie still watching other people step forward for tasks which would normally be ours. The Miracle of Receiving forced me to lay aside my ego and trust others. I guess for a man like me, to lay his ego aside was the real miracle, but the fact that others saw my needs through God's direction and came to my aid . . . that is a miracle worth recounting.

Retired Fire Department Battalion Chief John Fulco was one of the first friends to begin teaching me this concept. After over 26 years of friendship, John could talk to me about things no one else could mention. His wife Jana is a breast cancer survivor, so the Fulco's have first-hand knowledge of a lot of my challenges. One of those challenges—one I really did not want to talk about— was the economic struggle. This cancer caught me at a time when I had just tied a lot of my resources into a new business venture, so what little money I might have budgeted toward the medical bills had recently been spent. Also, because of my every-other-week treatment schedule, I was suffering a 50% pay-cut with my day job. Trying to juggle the loss of income with the new demands from hospital bills was overwhelming, especially after finding out how insurance works across state lines or what it really means when the insurance only pays their percentage of the bills. At one point, when things were pressing on us pretty hard, John said, "Let me help you."

I was taken back when he explained his plan. He wanted to raffle off a four-wheeler to raise money for my medical expenses. My first response was incredulous at best. I thanked him for what he was trying to do, but I insisted, "God is going to provide." This is when I say John began to teach me the Miracle of Receiving. I will never forget his reply: "God is trying to provide for you. He is trying to use me to provide."

Here I was, not wanting to receive help unless somehow it came straight from God when all the while God was the one trying to send me help. The correction struck me in both my mind and spirit: I was going to have to allow God to use people to help me with things I should be able to do on my own. So John developed this whole idea about a raffle. First, we contacted one of my cousins, Kenny McKinnon, who formerly owned McKinnon Honda in Texarkana. When I explained John's idea to him, he was excited to connect us with the right Honda rep. Then, he and John collaborated on the rest of the plans, and much to my amazement, after several months of tireless work with lots of volunteers, they raised tens of thousands of dollars to help with our medical expenses. I don't suppose I need to explain how it feels to go from wondering how on earth we were going to negotiate a payment plan with the hospitals, to seeing our bill whittled down to a more manageable size. But the main lesson learned is that I had to be willing to receive help from others. Regardless of my personality type, I was facing an economic struggle which I could not conquer on my own. I had to let others help me. John was instrumental in bringing me to that realization.

I mentioned the devastation which accompanied me the first day someone came to mow my lawn. This, too, was part of the lesson I was learning. Buddy Parker and John Miglicco, two other great buddies of mine, along with Dennis Aaron and his church family, came to me to tell me they were going to be mowing and manicuring my lawn until I was back in the saddle. I just did not know how to receive this news. First of all, I wasn't sure they knew what they were up against. After all, I have five acres, part of which I call a pasture so I won't feel obligated to mow it as nice as the lawn. Secondly, as I have already said, the thought of someone else mowing while I sat in the house was more than I wanted to think about. *Thank you, guys, but this is more than I can emotionally handle. I am a grown man. There are certain things I do as a grown man, and my yard is one of them.* That is as far as my thoughts could go at the time.

But now, my yard has never looked so beautiful! These guys did not care how I felt about their help; they insisted on doing what friends do. I have to say that this act of giving on their part forced me to take huge steps in my emotional and spiritual life. This is a miracle like I have never experienced in my whole

Christian walk. For people to come to me asking how they can help me through my trial is the opposite of how I have lived. I feel like I have always known how to give, but now I was learning how to receive. Today, even my "pasture" looks like a lawn. It is prettier than I could have done myself, and I could not be more proud to be on the receiving end of such a blessing.

You met Timbo in that horrible chapter on C-diff. He is the wiry ball of energy who helped me get some rest at the hospital by insisting the medical staff keep a sensible schedule. Well, he and his wife Theresa taught me even more about the Miracle of Receiving. Tim knows me well enough to predict what I would have said if he asked what I needed: "Well, Tim, the Lord is good and I'm doing fine. Thank you, but I can't think of anything I really need at the moment." So Tim bypassed me and said to Susan, "Had Durell not gotten this disease and started this treatment process, what is one of the projects you were planning at home?"

Susan has incredibly beautiful gardens, both vegetable and ornamental, in our back porch area. I built two raised beds for her, which she loves and tends to with the greenest thumb of anyone I have ever known (except her dad, a wonderful gardener). She always has a landscape project "in the works." When Tim asked Susan about any projects now delayed, she let him know about a rose bush transplant we had been planning. The next thing we knew, Tim was digging up seven rose bushes and transplanting them into the new garden space. This was no small task. He transplanted all seven rose bushes following strict gardening principles—weed prevention, mulching, even bordering—and made them just beautiful! Well, I walked outside while Tim was doing all this work, and of course, I ask, "What can I do? Let me help." Tim's answer rang with the Miracle of Receiving: "Yes, Durell, I do have something for you to do . . . You go inside, sit down and rest yourself. Let this medicine you are hooked up to do what it is designed to do! I am taking care of this garden." I have to say, this year those rose bushes all bloomed magnificently! All seven of them remind me of the Miracle of Receiving. Tim planted a garden, and I learned more of my lesson.

There were too many acts of kindness and gifts of service to mention them all. In Susan's accompanying chapter to this one, she lists as many as we could remember, although there is no way to list them all. But I have one more story to tell here as a part of this miracle of learning to receive. Perry and Stacy McDaniel, a husband and wife pair of captains on the Shreveport Fire Department, own a restaurant named Mel's Diner. They are wonderful people. Now, I could stay alive for a long time eating Ramen noodles or cheerios, but Perry wanted me and Susan to eat well even though we were facing challenges that could limit our restaurant outings. Perry gave Susan a yellow laminated card and said, "You and Durell come to Mel's and eat whenever you want to. This is something God wants me to do for you." After assuring Perry that I would never abuse the privilege of our special yellow card, I took him up on his offer (Pride is easily silenced by hot wings and hamburgers). So oftentimes, when I am between treatments, Susan and I eat at Mel's Diner on the house. "This is something God wants me to do for you." That is the lesson. Perry was giving for the Lord, and I was learning the Miracle of Receiving. It is no small thing to offer a big boy like me a card for free meals at your restaurant! Perry and Stacy offered us a part of their life's work, and for that, we are truly humbled and grateful.

As I was learning the Miracle of Receiving, the desire to give embraced me fully. Thinking of Susan, I wanted to say "Thank You" to her for the friend and companion she is to me. I planned a party of many of our close friends to honor her. All we could invite attended. They came from several different parts of the country to express their love and friendship to her. In the end, as I was elated receiving the outcome of my endeavors to support Susan, two of our close friends, Carl and Roy, surprised me by outgiving me. Thanks, guys. Once again, even in an effort to give,

I learned to receive. The list of those who have given in the Miracle is too long to write out, but the lesson God has emblazoned in my mind is that as we give to God, He always gives back to us at exactly the right time.

In this process of receiving, I look back over my shoulder and say, "Thank you, Lord, for bringing me to this place." I had never in my life been in the position of this type of need. I have always been healthy and able to do everything for myself. I have always been an energetic person, who lives for others. That is the life I enjoy. The Miracle of Receiving has come to me straight from the hand of God.

I speak with a lot of the cancer patients who see themselves as defeated because they cannot produce. I know that feeling well. I have wrestled with those emotions. However, the miracle is that God knows that emotion; He created it. He knows what it is like to be in a position of relinquishing authority to someone else. And when God relinquishes authority to someone else, to say, I give you authority to make decisions for your life, He allows that person to fail or succeed on their own. When I relinquish my authority to someone else, by allowing them to aid and assist me, I am saying, "I will back off, and you can do this yard any way you want to. You can do this flower bed any way you see fit." This frees me to receive what God wants to do in my life. It took a transformation of thinking. The Miracle of Receiving means that I am not the one producing; I am the one watching and receiving.

To say "No thank you" to the ones who offer help would be to say "No thank you" to God. In the kingdom of God, it is His desire to bless us, so as difficult as it may be for us with "Inspirer" personality types, let's not miss the Miracle of Receiving. God knows our needs. He knows the number of hairs on our heads. Throughout our lives, we have allowed God to use us to bless others, to work hard, and to accomplish tasks. Now, we have to allow God to use others to bless us! The Miracle of Receiving means that you have to let other people be experience the Miracle of Giving. With gratitude and humility, you have to appreciate their work for God and trust them to do it the best way they can. No longer are you asking God, "What can I do for others?" Now, you are asking him, "How do you want me to receive from others?" You have to learn how to say Thank You, both to God and to the people He uses to bless you. To receive help instead of offering help might feel like the antithesis of your life's calling, but you have to do what you have to do, and what you have to do right now is . . . learn to receive.

So many people have helped me learn this lesson; the stories I have related here are not by any means an all-inclusive list of blessings extended to me by others. They are just a sampling.

Because of my suffering, some people have had the opportunity to serve God like never before. They felt impressed by God to do an act of service for someone else in need, and then they felt the great joy of obeying His voice. When I first faced the humility of receiving from others, I wanted to stop them. I wanted to get done with this sickness and get back to work. Life even seemed out of control. However, now I see that it has all been under God's control. God is teaching me to embrace every leg of the journey because He is the great controller, and He has a great line-up of givers and servers on His team. Gratitude has now overtaken my resistance, and I am blessed to know that Living the Miracle means understanding the Miracle of Receiving. The treatment, sickness, and the loss of ego, all pales in comparison to the great blessing God has shown me in the Miracle of Receiving.

I would not have learned this lesson personally had I not had this journey. I knew this truth academically, but now I know it personally. Today I am more advanced in my understanding of how much God loves us, and how much He wants to take care of the needs in our lives and how willing and able the people of God are to hear the voice of God and to move on another person's behalf as unto the Lord. Wow! What a great miracle. I have learned to say thank you, not only to the Lord, but to the men and women of God who have given of themselves and their resources as God has laid the needs on their heart. I thank God I was able to learn the Miracle of Receiving even if it meant going through this cancer journey.

CHAPTER 15

BLESSINGS BEYOND MEASURE

by Susan Tuberville

My husband is a well-loved man. He is highly respected in his field of expertise, specifically trauma response and recovery. In his community, city, state, and—without stretching the truth—nationally, he has been called upon during times of disaster. I would not venture to say he is loved by everyone who meets him, but I would say it would be hard to find anyone who knows him who would have anything negative to say about him. God has blessed Durell with an outgoing personality, a spirit of compassion, and the ability to minister to people and help them through some of their darkest days. He has and is currently serving our city and parish in the role of chaplain for emergency service workers, which he has done for twenty-five plus years.

I mention all this because people were coming out of the woodwork to offer help. What can we do? Do you need money? Can I bring food, cut your yard, bring you firewood, work around the house, take care of your rental property? The list goes on and on. When God promises in his Word that if we will be faithful to Him with our tithe and first fruits then He will pour down from heaven blessings more than we can comprehend or think (Malachi 3 paraphrase)—HE MEANS IT! So much more than either of us could ever comprehend or think.

When people asked what they could do for us, we always responded with, "What we really need is prayer." **And did we ever get prayer support!!** Prayer from people whose lives Durell had touched—as a young high school student, a bible college student and dorm director, a youth pastor, a pastor, a chaplain to the fire department, a counselor, a chaplain to the sheriff's department, and a friend. More than we could comprehend or think! If there wasn't an immediate need, people pressed until they could find something, anything to show their love for Durell.

Although I hesitate to begin any kind of list here because it would be impossible to remember all the acts of kindness and love which poured out and are still pouring forth, I would feel remiss if I did not at least give you a glimpse of what this looked like for us.

Here are a few examples of how God has and continues to use His people to touch our lives during this difficult time:

- A high school reunion centered on happy memories and prayer—complete with DVD to share, organized by friends we had not seen in decades. This resulted in several reconnections made which have initiated mini-reunions, lunches, and long distance friendships reignited. Thanks, Brian, Kay, and Diane and all who attended.
- Food, from beef for the freezer, to homemade meals, to gift cards for meals, to a cookbook for meals specialized to chemo treatment. Thanks, Marc, Linda, Ms. Joyce, and so many others.
- Monetary needs were also met in many ways: a savings account set up at the Credit Union for people to make donations to help with medical expenses, a 4-wheeler was donated and raffled, a fundraiser at a local restaurant with a portion of proceeds directed toward Durell's medical care,

a poker run from the local Brother's Keepers motorcycle club, and many generous individual donations to help with costs incurred while Durell was out of work and medical expenses continued to flood in. Thanks, Terry and Pam, Sister Sharon, Patty and Mike P., Mark, and many others.

- Landscaping needs at home as well as at rental properties. This ranged from weekly yard care, to removal of dead trees, to stump removal, to building a rose bed, to a day of cleaning up after a storm blew through our area. Thanks, Tim and Ronnie and Open Range Fellowship.

- Maintenance at home including refinishing doors, capping a leaky brick wall, and driveway work. Thanks, Mark, Paul, and Rusty.

- The donation of the use of a vehicle for a more comfortable ride during the days of radiation. Thanks, Rusty and Lee.

- A Circle of Prayer unlike anything I've ever been a part of. Men and women from all branches of emergency service workers, whom Durell has worked with, joined together in one mission to pray for God to touch Durell and for His miracle power to prevail—and Wow, did it! Thanks to all who attended.

- Generous gifts of getaways for rest and recuperation for both patient and care giver. Thanks, Brian and Kathy, Terry and Pam, and Buddy and Karen.

- The gift of time from so many family members and friends—time spent visiting with Durell lifting his spirits, reminiscing, and just trying to keep his mind off the chemo he was receiving for

2 years of chemotherapy (many meals and chocolate shakes included)

- The gift of professional services offered from realtors, to massage therapists, to hair dressers
- The gift of encouragement through the ministry of cards and letters from literally hundreds of people that wanted to show their support (These were compiled in a 7 inch binder for Durell so that on days he needed some encouragement there was a tangible written record of the impact his life has had on so many, and the love they have for him)
- Durell has several people who send weekly encouragement through cards and phone calls. Thanks Shelia and Diedra.
- The gift of 'keeping in touch' through a special page on Facebook designed to give updates, request prayer, and give praise reports all from a dear friend we made while in Bible College
- The list goes on and on . . . our needs were met during our quarantined time in the hospital ranging from rolls of quarters for nonstop access to the vending machines, to cases of food, fruit, snacks, or anything we might need.
- A hotel room easily accessible for family for showers, naps, a complimentary breakfast daily for the last 11 days of Durell's hospitalization (an idea offered through a co-counselor and made possible by many brothers and sisters from the Shreveport Fire Department)
- The gift of time recording and transcribing as well as editing Durell's story into book format. Thank you, Patti and Brian.

My hope in mentioning some of these many gifts is to show how abundantly obvious it is—**This man is loved!**

Above all that we received from everyone was the amazing **gift of love**, the confirmation that indeed God would never leave us or forsake us—He was using His people to supply our needs!

I believe all this was possible because of the foundation and the love Durell has sown into so many lives through the years **and BECAUSE God's word is true!! He will give back to us— pressed down shaken together and running over, will he pour out from the windows of heaven, blessings more than we can comprehend or think** (Malachi 3; Ephesian3:20; Luke 6:38 paraphrase).

I also consider it a real life example of people putting into action the message Durell has preached untold times from God's word, "Greater love has no man than this, that he would LAY DOWN HIS LIFE for his fellow man."—**Not in the dying but in the living.**

How does one begin to say Thank You for such demonstrations of love? All I can think is to return it in kind. It is our hope and prayer that when the opportunity presents itself for us to be God's hands extended, we will continue to be in a position to act as so many friends and family members have for us.

Because… "Faith without action is not faith at all."

This is FAITH IN ACTION!

CHAPTER 16

THE MIRACLE OF PRAYER

Prayer is an amazing concept, an avenue for us to talk with God and allow God to talk to us. My journey through cancer has given me the opportunity to understand prayer more thoroughly as the ultimate connection God desires to have with us. Generally, when we think of prayer, we think of asking God for something and hoping He does it just the way we want. However, prayer means so much more than that. Yes, of course, prayer does bring specific answers according to God's promises, but I have also found that prayer teaches people about God and draws them closer to Him. I have also learned that praying for someone else can be as life-changing for the person praying as it is for the person being prayed for. The Bible says a lot about prayer. As you read through my thoughts on the Miracle of Prayer, please keep in mind I am coming from a Protestant, Evangelical, Full-Gospel approach, which is my chosen faith. Whatever your personal perspective on prayer, one thing is certain: Prayer is Miraculous. Prayer changes things. It brings us in line with the mind of God, where He can unveil His powerful promises to us and give us the faith to believe in them.

As I said, I do believe Prayer is attached to the Promises of God and His desire to bless us. During this battle with cancer, whether I have been praying for myself or holding on to the prayers of others, one promise in particular has always been close to my heart. At first glance, this promise might not seem related to cancer, but it is one of the biggest promises I have held on to during this time. Susan and I have always tried to be givers when it comes to tithes and offerings because we believe in God's promises about tithing (i.e., giving 10% of your income to God's work). Besides the promise to bless a tither financially, God adds that He will "protect them from pestilence" (Malachi 3). Wow. When I pray, I have this promise to hold on to. What does being "protected from the pestilence" mean to Durell Tuberville? It does not necessarily mean that cancer will go away (that is a bonus!). Rather, it means He will protect me from the pestilence of depression; He will protect me from the pestilence of hopelessness, uselessness, fear of the unknown, fear of dying, and being overwhelmed. Depression and the rest of these paralyzing emotions have tried at times to rule my mind. Chemotherapy, just plain yuck to say the least, can evoke a horrible gamut of emotional pestilence, but I choose to believe those feelings are the very things which God promised to protect me from in His promise to the tither. Prayer reminds me of this promise every day.

With this concentration on just one of God's promises, I reflect on the many times I have experienced the Miracle of Prayer throughout this time with cancer. On one particular Sunday in church, my Pastor, Denny Duron, asked me and Susan, along with a fellow minister Ricky Berlin and his wife Nancy, to come to the platform for prayer. At the time, Ricky had Multiple Myeloma (as of this writing, he has been declared cancer free. Praise God!). That morning Pastor Duron anointed us with oil and asked the congregation to agree together, praying aloud for healing in our bodies. They also prayed that our lives would impact others as we live this healing miracle. The impact of this congregational prayer on me was beyond words. Having my church family agree together and point their hands toward me and Ricky, had a tangible effect on me. I get chills again thinking about it. There we were with about 1100 people all lifting their voices in a roar of prayer. An atmosphere of love, praise, and power filled the room, and I could feel it all over my body. This changed my life! To feel the presence of God and the miracle of prayer happening through my church family, to look up and see all those people with their hands stretched forward was overwhelming. To hear their voices in an uproar of fervent prayer was like hearing a thousand-voice Gospel choir shaking the rafters. It was almost more than I could stand.

We have congregational prayer all the time. We anoint the sick with oil and pray for them as a church because we believe the promises of scripture (James 5), but this time was different because this time was for me! This time the prayer was for Durell, and the miracle of that congregational prayer was like a rushing mighty wind coming over me and Susan as we stood there. One of the reasons church is so important to us is because of the Miracle of Prayer. As people begin to pray in unison and agreement, it changes things. God hears and answers according to our faith in His Promises. If you don't have a church home, can I encourage you to find one? Please find a church that loves God, a church that wants to believe in the power and the presence of God. Attach yourself to them as your family in God. You need a group of people who can join you in the Miracle of Prayer. Whether your church is very small or large does not matter. What matters is that you have the support of others who believe in the same promises of God that you do.

As you can tell, I definitely believe in prayer's connection to God's promises, but I also believe the Miracle of Prayer is measured in other ways, for other purposes. One of those purposes is so people—especially people outside the church— will become aware that God is there! That may sound simple, but it is not. For too long in our country (from the late 60's to be exact), people have been abandoning their faith for "science," even to the point of posing the question, "Is God dead?" I want people to know God is indeed not dead, nor will He ever be. He is alive and real. I want them to know He answers prayer. They might deny His existence or their need for Him, but when they see me live the Miracle of Prayer, they will know that He is alive. I want everyone to know God intimately and to experience the Miracle of Prayer for themselves.

Take my grandsons, for instance. These little guys know we pray about *everything*. One time, I had two of my grandsons with me to shop for a used finishing mower. Tristan, the eldest of the twins, sat beside me in the truck. After we bought the mower and loaded it on the trailer, I said, "Boys, let's thank the Lord that He provided us this used mower we've been needing, and thank Him we got it for a price we were very happy with. The Lord provided the money for it, too." So we prayed, "Lord, thank you for the mower." Praying with Tristan and Jackson made the whole trip more significant. I want them to know that God is involved even in the small things of our lives like getting the right mower at the right price.

So my grandsons know we pray about everything in our family, yes, but the next part of the story is the point. When we got through praying, Tristan said, "Pop, we pray to Jesus for healing the bugs in you" (He learned from his momma, my precious daughter-in-law, Lindsay that Pop "has a bad bug"). To know that my grandson is trusting God and actively praying makes all this make sense. Then there is my youngest grandson, Creed, who always wants to know if I still have the "medicine thing" (the porta-catheter) in my chest. He puts his hand on it, rubs it and says, "Pop are they still putting medicine in there?" Then, we thank God together for giving these wonderful physicians and researchers such wisdom and knowledge to be able to help Pop fight this cancer. One day, I was finally able to tell Creed, "Well, this is the last time they'll have to put medicine in there" (it was the last time at the time). He wanted to know if it was because God had heard our prayers. You see? These grandkids have been praying for Pop, and God is doing a miracle. The foundation of prayer has been established in those children. They are praying every day and witnessing what God can do! Most of all, they are growing up knowing that they can communicate with God Almighty.

I am so excited that the Miracle of Prayer is being introduced in a way that my grandchildren understand. Even if it is through cancer, they are truly finding out how we "cast our cares on Him" (I Peter 5:7), and now they have a personal witness of what prayer does. They have seen it in Pop. Not long ago, I asked Susan as an educator, "Do you think the boys are old enough to remember that Pop had cancer and they saw the miracle of God?" "Absolutely," she said, "we can remember things from when we are five and six years old." My concern was—and my excitement now is—that they would always remember what God has done. This fight with cancer will build an unshakeable foundation in their young lives, a foundation which no one can steal from them. They will always know what the Miracle of Prayer looks like. My hope is that they will become powerful ministers of God, maybe not pulpit ministers, but living ministers because they know they knelt and prayed . . . they even took their little hands and anointed Pop with oil . . . and God did a miracle. Nothing can take that from them. They saw it. They know beyond a shadow of a doubt they witnessed what God can do with prayer. It is my prayer these boys will change and impact society for the glory of God. These boys will grow up with the foundation of knowing we can lay all our cares before God.

It is so refreshing to know that whatever number of days I have left, the seed has been sown for my five grandsons to know the Miracle of Prayer. Because of cancer, I have been able to be part of that foundation building. Wow! If I died today, I could die in peace knowing the legacy in my children and grandchildren is a solid understanding of the Miracle of Prayer. This Miracle of Prayer, however, has not stopped with just my church or my family. Countless acquaintances and contacts have been touched by the Miracle of Prayer. At the grocery store, the hardware store, the bank, or wherever else I may be, one of the first things I hear nowadays is "Durell, I am praying for you!" What a psychological and emotional lift it brings to hear this from so many! "I am praying for you" might be some of the most powerful words I have ever heard.

If my cancer has given thousands of people across the Ark-La-Tex and around this country a reason to talk to God, then I am proud to have done my part. Some people who might have been away from God for a while have returned to Him to ask Him to heal their old friend Durell. Businessmen from around my town, some who are not exactly known for their deep religious leanings, have stopped me to tell me they are now praying! Even outlaw bikers say to me, "Well, Preacher, for what it is worth, I am praying for you." To that, I say back to them, "It is worth everything!" Suddenly in those moments, I know this trial I have faced has been worth it! I tell those bikers, whom I have grown to know and love over the years in and out of their world as a chaplain and friend, "It is changing my life *because* you are praying!" The very thing I live for is coming to pass before my very eyes. Why would an outlaw biker ever pause to pray? Because his buddy Durell has cancer! Even if he simply whispers, "God, I don't know if you are listening to me, but if you are, would you touch Preacher Man?" Wow! How blessed am I? Had it not been for my cancer, these guys might not have prayed at all. Some of them might not have thought about God or ever had a tender moment with Him in their entire lives. Now, they are crying out to God for something. Some of them might even feel like they are just rolling dice on a bet that God might be there, but they are finding out He is. He listens to them and wants to have a relationship with them!

I was auctioneering not very long ago to raise some funds for the "I'm Still Me" burn camp, a camp for children who have been victims of burn accidents. The auction is held yearly in conjunction with a Brothers Keepers motorcycle rally (Brothers Keepers is a motorcycle club of professional and volunteer firefighters from all over the country). This rally is attended by all sorts of motorcycle clubs from the Bikers Against Child Abuse group (BACA), to the Gray Ghosts and Banditos, and of course the Brothers Keepers. To give you an idea of the size of this rally, it raised $50,000 for the "I'm Still Me" camp. During the rally this year, the national vice president, Perry McDaniel asked me to update everyone on my cancer condition because they all wanted to know how I was doing. Once more, from this sort of concern, I learned that thousands more around the country had been praying for me, each one now hoping to hear how my prognosis was playing out. Again, this represents the Miracle of Prayer — people were communicating with God.

In the middle of that auction, the national president, Marty Moss, walked over to Susan to express concern for me: "He has been at this for a couple hours now. Do you think he needs a break?" Susan said, "His heart is in this. He is not going to stop. He is going to do it till it's done." To be honest, Marty should have been right, but the Miracle of Prayer was at work in me at that moment. I wanted these people to see that what they had prayed for was coming to pass. I was going to serve God with all my heart on this day. I planned to give God all my energy, enthusiasm, and love for those children so that His glory would show through me. At the close of that auction, I did not know how exhausted I was until I got home because while there, I was on such a high, knowing that these compassionate people who were rallying for children were also rallying around me in the Miracle of Prayer.

In an earlier chapter, we talked about the Circle of Prayer that Ernest Mitchell put together around my house. This was the day all the service personnel and others encircled our house to see "the walls of cancer come down." Earnest's experience when the thought of this Circle of Prayer first entered his mind brings out another aspect of the Miracle of Prayer which I would like to explain from my perspective as a chaplain, counselor, and minister. I want everyone to understand that prayer is a two-way communication. One day, when Ernest was studying his Bible and praying, the passage about Jericho jumped off the page at him. You will remember this is the story where the Israelites marched around and around Jericho until the walls tumbled and crumbled. Well, Ernest had been praying for me because we are dear friends, but this day, God seemed to want to say something back. That's when Ernest heard an unction in his heart: "If you will circle that house, then the walls of cancer will come down." That is what God spoke to Earnest's spirit. Ernest had been seeking God, praying every day, and now he was faced with hearing God's voice in his heart and having to obey God's directive. This is an all-important aspect of prayer. God is not just looking for people who will talk to Him; He wants people who will listen and obey.

Oftentimes, we might wonder if God really speak to us. Unequivocally, the answer to that is Yes, God speaks to us! And, yes, God expects us to listen.

I need God to speak to me. When two formidable surgeons predict that even with treatment, the most I have is two years to live, then Yes, I need to know that God speaks to me. I begin to think about what God wants me to do with the number of days I have left. He gives me encouragement and direction. Sometimes, I want to say, "Why me?" but the Miracle of Prayer turns that around and I wind up asking, "Why not me? Why would I be any different from others who are exposed to the harsh elements of this world? Why wouldn't God be asking me to walk a hard road?" Life offers different crooks and turns to everyone; our job is to listen to God and find out how to navigate those dangerous spots. The Miracle of Prayer opens the doors of Heaven so that we can hear what the Bible calls the "still, small voice" of God.

God's Promises are real, and He wants us to believe in them. We are not trying to tell Him what to do by boldly coming to Him with requests, but we are standing firm by His promises, trusting Him to keep His word. My promise in prayer—Durell's end of the bargain—was that I will serve God regardless of the number of days I have left. If, like the doctors said, I really only had 700 days left, and if many of those days would be lived under the misery of chemotherapy, what was I going to do with them? How was I going to live for God? I had to address that for my own life. I had to listen for the voice of God to comfort me and encourage me down the right path. God, what is your directive while I have cancer? What do you want me to do with the next day—or two days, or maybe 700 days—which I get to live? The answers to these questions come from the Miracle of Prayer.

At this stage of the game, it looks like the miracle of prayer is manifesting itself in all these ways. People are seeing the power of God with their own eyes. Some are drawing close to God in prayer and faith for the first time in their lives. Some are finding out that God does speak to people and He wants to speak to them. Also, God's promises are as real to me and Susan today as they were the day I was first diagnosed. Finally, as of this writing (October 2014), the colorectal tumor—which was supposed to kill me or, at the very least, leave me with a permanent colostomy bag—has dissolved. Radiation was only supposed to shrink it enough to make the removal of my rectum easier, but with God, impossible things became possible. My colon and rectum have been restored. We will continue to monitor the specks of what seems to be cancer in my lungs, but the uptake of that cancer has been stifled as well.

God is the author and finisher of my faith. He is the Alpha and Omega, the beginning and the end. He is God whether I have cancer or whether I am cancer free. My role is to serve Him and follow His directives regardless of my circumstances. Living with cancer is a minor thing, not a major thing. To know that we are trying to please and honor God is a major thing. To know that we can pray . . . that is the greatest thing I know. Whether we approach him very quietly or boisterously, whichever method of prayer fits us, we can be confident God hears us from His throne of grace. Most importantly, He will answer us. That is what I call the Miracle of Prayer. Living the Miracle cannot be done without the Miracle of Prayer. More than anything, regardless of how this all ends, I want to hear the Lord say, "Well done, Durell, well done." When it is all said and done, one hundred years from now the world will not remember Durell Tuberville, but maybe somebody whom my story has touched will touch the lives of others until generations later, someone begins to walk with God at least in small part just because of what I have been through and how I went through it by the power of this miracle called prayer.

CHAPTER 17

THE MIRACLE OF PASSION

The day you hear the diagnosis, the day they find the big C, your whole system goes into shock. Wherever you are—in my case, I received the news over the phone—your heart drops, and the world stands still. You make all the necessary phone calls. You meet with your family. The shock eventually gives way to data collection, and life becomes a long list of questions. How do I handle this information? How do I prepare for what I don't even know may be coming my way? Automatically my mind began to race to all the things which are important to me, but somehow I left out a very important element. For a moment, fulfilling my own passions and desires seemed to shrink in comparison to the other emotions of love for family and uncertainty about the days ahead. However, I soon found out that a key to Living the Miracle was to keep being Durell, to keep focusing on the passions which make me who I am. Herein, I discovered an invaluable survival tool—The Miracle of Passion.

As I have said before, I quickly resolved the "Why me?" question with a heart-felt, "Why not me?" I live on the same planet as everyone else. I was very comfortable with the fact that I am a person living in a tough world. A lot of things in life thus far did not work the way that I wanted them to, and this episode was no different. I have always taken both success and failure as just a part of life's journey, each level preparing me for the next. When a business venture fails, I never think of it as a complete failure. Rather, I just see that somewhere I need to make an adjustment, reallocate my energies, or redefine my plan. Quitting has never really been an option. This is who I am. To change my regular mode of operation, now that it was my body failing instead of my business plan, would have caused me to crumble because it would not have been me. Part of beating this cancer would depend on how well I could still be me.

Of course not knowing what the future held or anything about chemotherapy or radiation was a challenge. I had no idea how long I was going to live, yet one of my core beliefs in life concerns the sovereignty of God. I had to ask myself whether or not God is really sovereign in the lives of His children, of whom I am one. If God is sovereign, then this trouble I am facing is part of God's direction and plan for my journey. So, therefore, how could I just give up or throw in the towel? Would I give up any other opportunity or challenge God tried to give me? Am I ready to face whatever I have to face in order to glorify God in my life? The question for me was and is, "How does God want me to live with this?" "How do you, God, want me to live in such a manner that when my life is over, those around me, especially those who are important to me—my spouse and my family, my staff and my friends—will see the example of character they would want to emulate?"

Once the shock of the diagnosis cleared, that's the passion which burned inside me again. The truth is that even before I had cancer, I had to ask myself these questions. My passion for life has everything to do with being what God wants me to be as an example and an encouragement to others. I want to love people, build relationships, start new businesses, help others succeed, and try new things. Having cancer did not change that passion. With cancer, I have an added passion. I want to leave people wondering what it is that allows me to live through this and still enjoy life. I want them to be encouraged and lifted up by my life. That is my passion.

I decided I could not lose that passion. I knew beyond a shadow of a doubt, if I lost that passion I would die. It would be the end of me physically. I am not afraid of dying, but if I die, I want to die with passion. After all, we are all dying one of these days. Cancer may not get me, but something will. I am not going to live for 200 years unless the Lord does something way out of the ordinary! If I die, I am going out doing the things I love to do for God — inspiring others and fulfilling others. I am going to die seeing somebody reach a goal which they would not have reached unless I encouraged them, blessed them, and sparked their vision, thoughts, and creativity. On my way out, somebody is going to feel better than they did before they encountered me. That passion is the sum of my life. It is who I am. Giving up that part of me would cause me to begin to die outside of God's design.

Regardless of whether or not you have cancer, when you lose your passion, a part of you begins to die. The temptation is to think about the obvious negatives. *I can't go to work anymore. I am going to feel bad all the time. I am going to be sick for a long time.* Those thoughts rob your passion for life, so we have to choose other thoughts. *Sure, I am going to be sick for a while, but I am not going to live sick! I am not going to hang my head and live the woe-is-me life. I am going to look for things I can do to retain the passion within me because passion plays a miraculous role in my life.* It can mean the difference between life and death. The difficulty of cancer is upon me, but I have to believe it is only for a season.

When I started taking chemotherapy, the doctors gave me a long list of possible of side effects. I read through them and noticed one side effect not on the list — death! To me, that meant LIFE was still an option! Somewhere, after all these potential side effects, there was going to be life (even if the doctors did still say, "two years max with treatment"). Passion for life began to rise up inside me. I was going to live this thing to the fullest whatever the fullest could be. When people would ask, "How are you doing?" I responded, "I am doing wonderful! I am <u>Living the Miracle</u>." Every day is another day to live for God; it is another day I get a chance to inspire someone, to help someone get close to God. That's my focus.

My pastor came to visit me in the hospital when I had C-diff, at one of the lowest points of my physical battle. He had one of those flip video recorders in his hand and said, "Durell, would you like to say something to the people at church?" At the moment, I honestly looked like death on a cracker. Pale, weak, and all puffed up from IV fluids, it is safe to say, I was not feeling well. I looked even worse than I felt. As the old folks used to say, I looked like the north end of a south bound donkey. You can imagine after lying in bed for about two weeks just how bad one can look. Talk about a major case of bedhead, I had it. I looked like Larry on the Three Stooges, or worse. I had a nasal cannula to supplement oxygen, and here my pastor was wanting to do a video for the church to watch. But a passion rose up inside me reminding me of my determination to inspire others. As he filmed the video, I talked about keeping the focus on God and Godliness no matter the situation. My passion to inspire their faith drove me on. I wanted them to see how God can sustain those who love Him even in difficult times.

Pastor showed that video at church on the big screen! Susan saw it and could not believe he showed it. She talked about my hair, the hospital gown I had on, and how "out of it" I was with all the medications and pain I was in (All these things are important to our wives, but not so important to us husbands at times. Maybe they should be more so). But in the end, my passion overrode everything else, and the whole church was inspired to press through their own trials and to pray for me even more.

I know it was not easy for Jesus when he said, "If it is possible, let this cup pass from me. Nevertheless, not my will but yours be done." However, the passion of knowing what he was accomplishing pushed him forward. I want to have the mindset and passion of Christ, to look at what lies ahead and still say, "Let's rock and roll!" Well, he might not have said, "Let's rock and roll," but that's what the passion inside me repeats over and over.

I remember having the discussion with Dr. Bob when he explained to us just how the chemotherapy would drain my strength. He said it would cause me to feel weak and possibly lose weight. When we got home, Susan said to me, "Durell, you are going to have to rest," but I said, "I am not sure what that means. Tell me what that means." She said, "You can't go as much as you have been going." Then I wondered, "Who is it that is supposed to regulate how much I can go and do? If I lay down, all the air is going to go out of me." I just could not lie down. I had to get up and do something, regardless of what was going on. At that point, I called a buddy of mine who was also going through cancer. I went to high school with Stacy. He was a defensive end of our football team, a big burly guy who went on to play for Northwestern State University. He was a standout ball player and a great guy. I called big Stacy and said, "I heard you got cancer like I have." He said, "Yep, I heard you got it, too." We talked about cancer for a few minutes and then I got to the real question, "Man, does your infusion therapy knock you down?" Stacy is about 6'3", probably weighing about 280 pounds. His answer was full of passion and all I needed, "Naw bud, I just put on my overalls and go to work. Nobody even knows I got it on." He had a subclavian porta catheter like mine.

Stacy inspired me. In reality, my treatment did knock me out during the infusion week, so I could not "put on my overalls and get to work" the same way Stacy did. However, I figured out what I could do. I would get so tired when the infusion pump was on that there was no way I could do my counseling job, so I planned all my counseling appointments on my non-infusion week. I would work my heart out with my passion full throttle during the times I knew my energy was high. I was not going to lose my vision and passion because vision and passion are what keep me going. Remembering I am still alive, I am still a man, and I am still able to fulfill what is inside me; these are my passion. So that is what I choose to do. To get up, when I don't have the infusion pump on and go to work.

Even on the days I was on the infusion pump, I decided I was still going to live. So that is when I went on lots of excursions with friends. As seen in the chapter on the Miracle of Friendship, we ran errands, took trips, fished, hiked and did lots of hanging out. I wanted to be as active as I could, so these guys came to "babysit" me as often as they could. After I learned from a friend of mine who had survived breast cancer that eating a lot helps counter the negative effects of chemotherapy, I started cooking breakfast for the guys who would come over to keep me occupied. I was able to add that to my list of passions (For the record: she said I should eat lots of times during the day, not lots of food at one time). My friends appreciated the breakfasts, and I appreciated the friendship. John, Buddy, Ernest, Dewain, Leland, Mark C., David and Mark R. all helped me keep some passion going.

I did learn the value of a good nap, but even that became related to my passion. I am not a "nap guy." However, now I would give out in the middle of the day, so I finally decided just to try it to see what happens. I closed my eyes and fell asleep in the middle of the day! Taking naps was not part of my life's passion, but it became part of my journey. You see? My family is my passion, and as it turns out, the evening time is when my family was at the house. Whether it was Susan home from work or whether the kids and grandkids stopped over to see Pop, if I allowed myself to nap during the day, then I could be my complete self for them in the evening. The passion to stay involved in their lives meant that I had to start taking a nap so I could have the energy to be up and be with them at night. Playing with grandsons is a passion worth living for.

I have a passion for whatever my children and grandchildren are doing. Just before I was diagnosed with cancer, I had helped my son Dustin break ground on a new restaurant in Texarkana, about an hour and a half away from my house. One thing that helped keep my passion going was the times a friend and I would jump in the car to see the progress of the construction. I remember Ernest asking me once, "Man do you feel like doing this? Texarkana is a long way." I said, "I have to go! That's what keeps me going!" Talking to the guys on the building crew, checking in on Dustin, helping him pursue this dream, these made up the passion that made survival a possibility. I might be able to stop for a nap, but if I stopped doing the things I loved all because I had cancer, then cancer would have beaten me.

Keeping the passion is part of the success of Living the Miracle, not giving up, not allowing yourself to lose your dream whatever that dream may be. Do not give your passion away to cancer; don't give it away to illness. Do not give your dream away to feeling bad today. Hold on to it! Pursue your passion. Even if you can only pursue it one inch at a time, pursue it that one inch. Tomorrow you can pursue it six inches, then a foot, and then a mile. But don't give up on your passion. The Miracle of Passion inside you is always yours to keep. It is something that is going to help you even when you do not feel like continuing. Part of what I hope to achieve with this book is to encourage you, if you know somebody who has been diagnosed with cancer or you yourself have been diagnosed with cancer, to pull up the passion that moves you and defines you. Find it! Pursue it! Think about it! Dream about it. Plan for it! Envision it!

Several years before I was diagnosed with cancer, Dr. Bob referred one of his patients to me. Let me close with her story. She had been diagnosed as terminal, already in active dying. She had a very short prognosis, only about four months. By the time she came to me, she was exhausted, completely worn out. Her life revolved around taking chemo, with about two days every other week that she felt "ok." I asked her what her passion was, to which she quickly and easily replied, "My husband and my daughter." We immediately turned our focus to her passions. Her husband: she wanted to do things for him, to love him and spend time with him. What was her passion for her daughter? To see her daughter accomplish her own dreams and to be with her for her extracurricular activities. Her daughter was about 11 at the time.

We looked closely at the calendar and discovered that she could count on about four days out of the month, two days every other week that she would feel like getting out and doing something. The chemotherapy made the other days impossible for her to really focus and function. With this understanding, we started a new game. From now on, she would identify every moment where her mind was clear enough to think, and in those moments, she would think about her passion. Then, even though she was too low to accomplish anything physically, she would plan out what she would like to do on the two good days. One of those days, she would plan how to fulfill her passion with her husband, and the other day she would plan things to do with her daughter. She planned twelve days' worth of things to do with her two passions.

She finished her life following that cycle. After she died, her husband contacted me because he wanted to say thank you. He wanted to tell me how much his wife had enjoyed her two days, every other week. They had great fun together, living out those last four or five months of her life, two days at a time. One day was his; one day was their daughter's. She would spend each of her days exclusively with the people she was passionate about. She died never losing her passion, and her family remembers that they were the objects of her passion. She had planned out a variety of things for them to do together and they enjoyed every memory of it. She died happy and content, fulfilling her passion. Did cancer take her life? Yes, it did, but it never took her passion.

To Live the Miracle, you must have the Miracle of Passion.

CHAPTER 18

THE MIRACLE OF COURAGE

Volumes have been written about courage. Stories of courage give us chill bumps and bring tears to our eyes. Our heroes are made of it. They face their fears and plow forward toward their goals. They win championships or save lives with a full supply of what we call courage. When people overcome great odds or stare down some insurmountable challenge, we always admire this one quality: courage. I have faced a debilitating disease and have fought with all my might to beat it, but when I think about the courage in my story, it is not my own which I am impressed with. The cancer patient does need an awful lot of courage to make it from day to day, but the real courage lies in the heart of the caregivers. The faithful spouse, the resourceful friends, the patient partners, and so many others who drive the story to its glorious conclusion: these are the heroes. These are the ones who deserve the badge of courage.

To live with someone who has cancer, to face the daily struggle of possibly losing them, to care for them when they are completely unconscious of your sacrifice, these are the marks of true courage. I have been the recipient of this type of courage. Susan is the most courageous person I know. She has been the perfect example of a tireless caregiver. The spouse of the cancer patient is going to see them at their absolute worst, throwing up, suffering from diarrhea, and succumbing to a long list of side effects from treatment. I have passed out, and Susan found a way to help me. I have been contagious with a very dangerous bacterial infection and should have been quarantined away from her for her own protection, but Susan threw caution to the wind and took care of me anyway.

The courage of commitment found in the spouse who toughs this sort of situation out is the kind of courage real marriage is made of. Marriage is not about infatuation in some sort of Hollywood love. Marriage is the opportunity to complete our lives and become everything God has designed us to become. Marriage presents us an opportunity to become a complete person. If we stay committed to marriage long enough, it will force us to develop the passion and compassion that God wants us to have in all of our interpersonal relationships. Marriage is not about whether your spouse does everything right all the time. It is about living through the failures, living through the difficulties, and even living through the poor decisions. Marriage is about the fun, it's about enjoying the passionate moments we have together. It's about the sense of fulfilling our individual passions and sharing those moments with the person we have chosen. It is about choosing to fulfill their passions because we know what their passions really are. This is the courage of marriage. I thank God to have had a courageous spouse through this process. I don't know how effective I would have been had I not had Susan. As you read earlier, she did not just take care of me and my ailments, but she also took care of things at home and the office during several weeks when I was incapacitated.

Susan is indeed my hero. It is important for those of us who are cancer patients to find a way to encourage our spouses and tell them Thank You. If you cannot muster strength for anything else, at least get a word out to show you appreciate your spouse's sacrifice. Without your spouse, you would be in most of this battle by yourself. It is a horrendous battle not to be self-centered when you are the one with the cancer. After all, you do not feel good. You have learned the patterns of treatment enough to know when you are going to feel bad all over again, and again, but that is why you have to find the courage in the times you feel good to thank your spouse for his or her courage during the times that you feel so bad. The value of the committed spouse cannot be measured. Let them know you know this.

I have also had the privilege of having courageous friends and family. I have seen true courage on display by those who don't avoid me. Discomfort or not knowing what to say can often keep good people from doing good things, but courageous friends and family step through this discomfort and ask how I am or what they can do for me. Courageous people have gathered around me, staying close, spending time with me, laughing with me about my calamities, my bowel issues, my feet issues and my other cancer-related troubles. The miracle of having courageous friends has repeatedly demonstrated itself through my cancer journey. In the chapter of the Miracle of Friendship, I tried to list several courageous friends. Many others displayed great courage as well. People like Patti Bornaman who works with me as a colleague and friend and who has even helped me in writing this book displayed great courage by sticking with me as part of my staff. Patti held the fort down in the counseling services while still finding time to visit me in the hospital and volunteer to help in any way she could. Patti even washed our laundry one day and took care of some other looming needs for us because we were bound to the hospital. To have courageous friends is such a blessing.

Courageous friends like Tim Thames, Reggie McElhannon, Carl McBeath, and my lifelong bud John Kellogg, all stayed with me at the hospital when I had C diff. They knew I was contagious, but their courage won out. The Lord said he would protect us if we have to go to places where we might encounter peril and disease, and these friends trusted His promise. They lived the courage of this promise from God. Guys whom I love dearly were courageous enough to live the Miracle of Courage for no other reason than to demonstrate their friendship in the greatest time of need. My courageous friend David Glass visited the hospital almost every day.

Craig Kennedy, my Chief Administrative Officer and Office Manager for Personal Solutions, Inc. is another example of great courage. He is one of my heroes. He stepped up and managed one of our businesses to keep it afloat. He had to make a lot of hard decisions which, prior to my becoming sick, were not decisions he had to face, yet he stepped up at a moment's notice. Craig took the captain's helm and ran the ship without wavering. His courage said, "I will make the decisions and do the things necessary for us to keep going at such a time as this." Many in his position might have been afraid to make of potential mistakes, afraid to fail or mess something up beyond repair. Many lesser men would have chosen to go to work somewhere else, but Craig proved his courage.

Our boys demonstrated the Miracle of Courage to leave their work places and families in order to come to their dad's side. Their courage has made me proud. I could not even respond at the time to let them know, but I was amazed by their courage under these dire circumstances.

We can't overlook the Miracle of Courage in this journey of Living the Miracle. Courage spurs people on to come to our rescue. Without it, we would be fighting all alone. Far more courageous are all of these folks than those of us who live with cancer. The cancer has been forced on us, and we really don't have a choice whether to live with it or not. Our friends and loved ones, on the other hand, do not *have* to live with the cancer. If they wanted to run from it, they could, yet they choose to walk with us. They choose to stick it out and be here for us. Believe me, fear tries to discourage them as much as it attacks you and me, but they have chosen to demonstrate the Miracle of Courage on our behalf. Thank God for the Miracle of Courage.

CHAPTER 19

A NEW REVELATION OF
COURAGE AND FAITH

by Susan Tuberville

I have been a Christian since I was twelve years old. In my
opinion, a Christian is not one who knows about God, but
rather one who knows God, knows what sacrifice he made on the
cross and chooses to follow Christ in character. I have known
about God and his son Jesus as long as I can remember. Raised in
a United Methodist Church, I was baptized at seven years old.
However, when I was twelve, I made a decision at youth camp
not only to know about God or to know about Christ, but also to
know Christ. I desired a relationship with Him; I wanted Him to
be Lord of my life. From that point on, my relationship with Jesus
as my Lord has grown. When I think of this transition in my
young life, the scripture from First Corinthians comes to mind,
"When I was a child, I spoke as child, I thought as child, but when
I became a [woman] I put away childish things" (Paraphrased).
This transition from knowing about God to knowing God would
mark who I am for the rest of my life. It has been a long time since
I made that decision to become a mature Christian. I still don't
think I have "arrived," but I have certainly come a long way.
There is so much yet to learn, but when I gave my life to Christ, I
felt as though, overall, I was putting away childish things and
growing in my faith to become like Him and to know Him.

I believe in faith. I live by faith, and I try to practice and share my faith with others. However, throughout this journey of Durell's fight with cancer, I learned how little faith I have actually practiced. The concepts of faith and courage have landed in my spirit like brand new revelation. Here I was, a grown woman and "mature Christian," facing a need for faith and courage like I had never known. Would I find it? One thing was for sure, Durell certainly had it. He had enough for both of us, but I still wanted mine.

Even now as I would beat myself up over my short comings, I have only to remember the story of Jesus and his disciples in a small boat on the water in a storm. It was a storm the disciples could see no way out of—they were scared. No, not scared, they were terrified! But where was Jesus? Why was he not on the deck with them worrying about the waves and the wind which seemed to be overtaking them? He was there on the boat with them during this fierce storm, but at the point of their greatest fear, they found him sleeping below deck. His followers were scared beyond measure, but he was asleep. When they woke him up in their panic and fear, they questioned him with accusation, "Master, do you not care that we perish?" At that point, Jesus admonished them with words which all of us need to hear: "Oh you of little faith, how long have I been with you and you still don't get it." Then he commanded the storm to be still. "Peace," he spoke to the storm. "Be still," He said to the wind and the waves. And Peace followed his command. Peace settled on the waters, but most miraculously, peace also found its way into the hearts of his followers.

In September of 2012, I found myself and my husband, our whole family, on a boat in the middle of a storm. The waves of uncertainty, the winds of pain and treatment and physical limitations were mounting around us in this storm called Cancer. I would definitely say all of us on this boat are believers in the Master. I would even dare to say we are his disciples. I think I can speak for my family when I say we all believe that Jesus is "in control." However, the fear from the wind and waves can reveal a lot about where we really are in our faith. I was scared even though Jesus was on the boat. I feel as though I can hear him asking of me, "Oh you of little faith, how long have you walked with me, and you still don't truly 'get it'?"

My husband, this man of God, this patient of cancer, gets it. He has faced the medical experts, the radiologists' reports, the physical trials that would bring most of us down, and he has always faced them with Faith. He has the kind of faith that moves mountains. The Bible says, "Faith is the substance of things hoped for, the evidence of things unseen" (Hebrews 11:1). Durell holds a true understanding of this kind of faith; he understands the **substance of things hoped for**. You can hear it every time he answers a new challenge, "Yes, but God . . . !" He understands the **evidence of things unseen**. We are Living the Miracle as a testament to Durell's faith in the things unseen.

Oftentimes during this storm, I felt emotions that were in direct conflict with this faith. After all, I had seen the evidence of MRI's, CT's, PET scans, and radiologists' reports, but Durell had the evidence of things "unseen"—God's promises, God's power. As born-again believers, we believe in the power of the spoken word. The Bible often exhorts us to "speak" to the mountain in order to see it removed. Durell has been speaking to this mountain, this disease, from day one. His words are always prefaced with introductions like, "The good news is..." or "I'm just living the miracle, brother." This has been his response to cancer, a response befitting the courageous faith he embodies.

As his wife and the mother of his sons, I was often conflicted with the information he presented to our boys. You might remember from an earlier chapter that while Durell would speak from his own "faith" perspective, I wanted to "shoot straight" with my sons. After all, they are not children to be protected from the truth; they are men. They are good, strong men. They are God-fearing men, and they are solid in their own faith. The sad reality of it is that I needed their strength. I did not want to diminish Durell's "faith," so instead of bringing my weakness to him, I often took it to my sons.

God—and Durell—taught me through this journey what real faith looks like. They have taught me that there are levels of faith and I have a long way to go before I reach the faith which God intends for me to have. I am thankful to have had all these years with Jesus as my savior. I am thankful to have had all these years as the wife of this mighty man of God. I know better than most his shortcomings and the things he struggles with, for he too is far from perfect. However, lack of faith in God is NOT one of Durell's weaknesses. I am thankful for the revelation of what Faith is and the example I have of how it is lived out in front of the world. My faith has been challenged, but it has grown through this journey.

I felt the Peace that Jesus spoke to our storm when we received the word that there is no more tumor, the lymph nodes are inactive, and the lung nodules are stable! At this news, we rejoiced. Miraculously God's peace settled in the hearts of my family as we felt Him speak to our storm. Still today, we rejoice over the news of "clinical remission"; however, I don't think it was "news" to Durell. He was not surprised in the least. After all, he had been "Living the Miracle" every day.

And as for me, this new revelation of faith and courage resounds in my heart . . .

Every Single Day is a Miracle, LIVE IT!

During our journey, I came upon a song by Bruce Springsteen which I have fallen in love with. How on earth I have gone all these years without listening to "The Boss," I still don't know, but I do know this song has touched me in a special way. At first it spoke to me of waiting for my husband while he recuperated, that no matter how long it took, even if his hand slipped free, I would wait, until such a time as we could again travel side by side. But lately its meaning has shifted. I now see that Durell is the one walking ahead. His faith, his strength, is still leading me, and all too often he has to wait for me as I fall behind!

I wanted to share these lyrics as a final statement of thanks to Durell because just as the lyrics say, he has made his steps clear that I may see, and my faith is growing as I try to catch up!

"If I Should Fall Behind"
Lyrics by Bruce Springsteen

We said we'd walk together baby come what may
That come the twilight should we lose our way
If as we're walking a hand should slip free
I'll wait for you
And should I fall behind
Wait for me

We swore we'd travel darlin' side by side
We'd help each other stay in stride
But each lover's steps fall so differently
But I'll wait for you
And if I should fall behind
Wait for me

Now everyone dreams of a love lasting and true
But you and I know what this world can do
So let's make our steps clear that the other may see
And I'll wait for you
If I should fall behind
Wait for me

Now there's a beautiful river in the valley ahead
There 'neath the oak's bough soon we will be wed
Should we lose each other in the shadow of
the evening trees
I'll wait for you
And should I fall behind
Wait for me

Darlin' I'll wait for you
Should I fall behind
Wait for me

CHAPTER 20

THE MIRACLE OF REMISSION

September 28, 2012 looms in my mind more than any other date, yet May 2014, has become one of the best months of my life. I have always loved May because that is when Susan and I were married, but May has also become the memorable month when we first heard the words "Clinical Remission" as a possibility. We had prayed for 21 months all the while keeping the mantra, "Living the Miracle." Suddenly, after months of bleak reports, there was now a chance of remission. This date is obviously very special to me because it marks the moment I was able to set my sights beyond the short life span which the doctors had originally predicted. The reason my sights had not been set so far out is easy. Our mantra was not, "I will one day have a miracle;" rather, we declared every day, "I am Living the Miracle." There's a big difference between the present and future tense, and the way I saw it, I was Living the Miracle every day, regardless of whether I ever reached "remission" or not. I hope that point resonates with every person who has heard my story. That is the real reason I wrote this book.

God is still in the miracle business. He was working a miracle the very day I received my traumatic diagnosis. As you read earlier, the events leading up to and confirming my diagnosis were nothing short of sovereign. Divine timing and coincidences, which could only have come from Heaven itself, guided us through the unknowns, leading us to the right doctors at the right stages of the process. Living the Miracle was not only about finally reaching remission, but it was also about getting the diagnosis right.

After the Miracle of Diagnosis, when we actually began declaring that we were "Living the Miracle," we would never allow our faith-focus to make demands on what the miracle should look like. Sure, we stood on God's promises of complete healing, but frankly, I was ready to stare death in the face and tell him I still believe in the God who heals, even if I did not get "healed." Even though I knew God can and will heal cancer, I could not set my mind on that kind of healing as the only element of "Living the Miracle." If remission and healing had been our demands upon God, as if we were holding His feet to the fire until He did what we wanted, then we would have missed out on the many other miracles which you have read about in this book. Because of this, I never focused on a future day, or even the desire for a future day, when I would hear a physician say, "We can't find any more cancer in your body!" For me, I felt that that kind of approach to faith would actually obstruct the day-to-day focus of being the best I could be, of making the most of every moment's opportunities. For my miracle, I needed each "today" to be *the* day I was Living the Miracle, whether or not I ever heard the doctor declare me "cancer free." Living the Miracle meant getting through every stage of the process bringing glory to God and serving Him whole-heartedly.

As long as I live, I will never forget the Miracle of Treatment. An immediate healing would have been nice, but the treatment itself proved miraculous at every level. As just one example of the many treatment miracles, one day an inconclusive biopsy report made the doctors scratch their heads, and I was tempted to let this deter me from my confidence. However, I had decided to trust these doctors and live the Miracle of Treatment, letting God receive glory from the medical world which He had inspired. Since they were not sure of what to conclude from the biopsy, the doctors thought it would be best to keep fighting it as if it were cancer, so I said, "If that seems right to you, then hit me with both barrels. Give me everything you've got, and let's aggressively beat this!" Throwing myself into the Miracle of Treatment, I even suggested the idea of gamma knife radiation for these unidentifiable nodules. Whatever miraculous treatment was available, I wanted it tried on me. I soon found out, though, that I needed a miracle just to make it through that treatment. During the radiation to the lungs, I had to lie on my back with my arms over my head, sometimes for two hours. It was painful, but in the process of treatment, God gave me the miraculous idea to sing my way through it (after Lamaze-type breathing had failed to help me). Now, what I did not think about was how the hospital staff had to endure my bellowing (yes, my singing is more like bellowing . . . like a cow giving birth). Afterward, they all reported that they had enjoyed my "music," so as you can see, the Miracle of Treatment did not fail. Those radiation techs got a "blessing" from it, and I am alive today, living on this side of the dirt, because of the Miracle of Treatment.

Then there was the Miracle of a Dream, my pastor's dream which woke me up with a new revelation of trusting God instead of myself. Because of this prophetic dream, I began to find self-worth in something other than my own performance. Add to that the Miracle of surviving C-diff, along with the Miracles of the Prayer Circle and of individuals' Prayers by the thousands, and you get more of the invaluable pieces of this "Living the Miracle" puzzle. Furthermore, my journey was also paved by the Miracle of a Supportive Spouse, the Miracle of Friendships, and the Miracle of Family. Without those miracles, the mantra "I am Living the Miracle" would never have been worth repeating. Passion, Courage, and Learning to Receive are also miracles which I am now living in a brand new way because of this fight with cancer. This story closes with the Miracle of Remission, but that is plainly not the whole miracle. I am still Living the Miracle today because every "today" has become a miraculous day for me to do my best for God.

Back to the beginning of the end of this story, in the early part of May, I went to see Dr. Bob. In late March or April of 2014, he had ordered a series of scans which revealed I was doing very well and was responding well to treatment. However, after each of these scans he would never say, "There's no more cancer," and he never used the word "remission." Throughout the chemotherapy and radiation processes, these types of reports were normal. My body was responding well, and since I was not having a lot of side effects and my attitude seemed right, we would always keep fighting according to the plan. The doctors would remind me from time to time to exercise and eat moderately, but the idea of a full recovery or a long, healthy future never entered the prognosis. They never tried to promise me that what they were doing, or anything I could do, would guarantee remission. I never felt like there was any "one thing" out there that was going to automatically bring a cure. Honestly, this approach was good for me because it helped me just to put my head down and push forward with whatever the physicians' directives might be for each next step. I simply learned to trust God and keep moving.

Finally, we had moved along to this day in May, when Dr. Bob came in with his new report. Unlike all the times before, he had a brighter little glimmer of hope. This is when he mentioned the word I had never heard: clinical remission. We might not be there just yet, but it seemed not to be impossible.

After the next radiation treatments, Susan and I had another visit with Dr. Bob. Another set of scans revealed, in Dr. Bob's words, ". . . there is no rectal tumor, nothing in the lymph nodes, and . . . the nodules in your lungs are stable." I listened very intently to this new language, which I had never heard. Then I asked the question, "Dr. Bob, can we now use the word 'remission'?" His response ends this chapter with the glory I felt that day: "Absolutely, we can say that you are in clinical remission." Out of sheer joy that God had done this work in me, I began to cry. The miracle of healing is now on medical record.

The miracle I want to share with you is that God sustained me through it all. Not only is the cancer healed, but through this journey, God has touched my spouse and my children, my coworkers, my friends, and my extended family. They have all witnessed the presence of God. All the people who have prayed for my healing can now say "Amen and Praise God!" Stage 4 Cancer, with its bleak and ugly prognosis of death and certain bodily destruction, has now been healed.

In all my life, I have never had so many people tell me I look good! I told one lady, "I must have really looked bad before I had cancer because so many people tell me I look good now." Most people expected me, especially during treatment, to look horrible, sick, ashen, and blanched. God has been gracious; sometimes, as noted earlier, I thought I looked like death on a cracker, but God somehow made me look good to others.

All I can definitely say throughout this process and at the time of this remission report is that God has sustained me the entire journey. I am careful to say only what the Doctor says, but it has become a constant joy to repeat it—"I am in clinical remission." Is the fight completely over? Well, we still have to observe my body every three months through a series of scans to make sure nothing reappears. But am I afraid the cancer will reappear? No, sir . . . I am happy to die, and happier still to live and bring glory to God almighty. "For me, to live is Christ and to die is gain" (Philippians 1:21).

I would encourage you if you know of anyone who has cancer, please assist them not to focus on the end result, but rather on what they can be today. If you are reading this book and you are on a cancer journey yourself, remember this. Even before your diagnosis you knew you would not live to be 200. You knew life would come to an end. We have all talked about it, especially when dying applies to others, but we never want to face it ourselves. If you have heard the words, "You've got cancer," then you know the big "C" can bring you a realistic outlook on the end of life. Trust God every day as if it is your last and at every new day, you will be encouraged that yesterday was not the end. You still have today. For me, they said Stage 4, so living each new day was a miracle in itself. The Miracle of Remission turned out to be icing on the cake.

The journey of our lives, regardless of what we encounter, is best walked when our focus turns away from the difficulty of the situation toward the God who sustains us. How can we be the best we can be through whatever situation we are in? I am telling you that you can Live the Miracle in your life. You can still love life and all of those around you. You can still Live the Miracle by proclaiming to the world, regardless of the diagnosis, "I am Living the Miracle." God was with me and God wants to be with you. To God be all the glory.

Thank you for following my journey. Now, join me in "Living the Miracle!"

CONCLUSION

It is October 21, 2015 and I am going to publishing with this book. I do not however want to leave you without describing where I am in this miraculous journey of cancer.

To-date I still have metastatic disease in my lungs. My clinical remission lasted until December of 2014 when the cancer in the lungs began to show growth. Dr. Bob determined it was necessary to begin another treatment regimen of chemotherapy. And so, I have been receiving treatment to stop the growth of cancer in my lungs.

As of today's date, my cancer is "stable" and the growth has stopped. I think this is the first occasion in my life I have been called "stable." However, the miracles of God continue daily in my life and in the lives of those around me. The new treatment modality is considered "maintenance" of the diseased lungs and is a smaller dose of a less powerful combination to keep the disease at bay.

Life is still about how God wants me to live for Him through the continued journey of cancer. The prayer continues for complete healing. Life is still worth living and living the miracle we will do.

Susan and I have adopted a new practice of going someplace we have never been and doing something we have never done between chemo periods. At the end of a cycle, 18-20 weeks, we complete this practice. I would encourage you to create something to look forward to as often as possible. This sustains hope and encouragement throughout the cancer treatment journey for both patient and care provider.

Calendar visits with family and extended family, with friends and neighbors, with church and community groups to get the focus off the treatment cycle and on to Living the Miracle in your life too.

I am so grateful to have the opportunity to share my story with you and that you would take the time to read it. I pray that my journey will encourage you in your journey. Please begin to count the miracles in your life, write them down in your journal, and talk about them with your family and friends. Live your Miracle as Susan and I continue to live ours.

God Bless You,
J. Durell Tuberville
Living the Miracle

ABOUT THE AUTHOR

Dr. J. Durell Tuberville is licensed as a Professional Counselor and Marriage and Family Therapist. He is President of Personal Solutions, Inc. and owner of Trinity Mediation and Associates and Trinity Property Management, LLC. He serves as an Associate Pastor at Shreveport Community Church and is Chaplain of the Caddo Parish Sheriff's Department. He is currently living through Stage Four Rectal Cancer with his wife, Susan. The Tuberville's have two sons, Josh and his wife Claleigh, Dustin and his wife Lindsey, and five grandsons, Jackson, Cash, Tristan, Eli, and Creed.

CPSIA information can be obtained
at www.ICGtesting.com
Printed in the USA
FSOW01n1833291215
15076FS